Managing Adult Inmates

Classification for Housing and Program Assigments

by Herbert C. Quay, Ph.D.

This publication may be ordered from:
American Correctional Association/4321 Hartwick Road, Suite L-208
College Park, Maryland 20740 (301) 699-7600

This project was supported by Grant FB-6 awarded by the National Institute of Corrections, U.S. Department of Justice. Points of view or opinions stated in this publication are those of the American Correctional Association and do not necessarily represent the official position of the National Institute of Corrections or the U.S. Department of Justice.

Cover design and graphics by Alonzo L. Winfield III.

Copyright © 1984, American Correctional Association
ISBN 0-942974-64-6

The reproduction, distribution, or inclusion in other publications of materials in this book is prohibited without prior written permission from the American Correctional Association.

NATIONAL INSTITUTE OF CORRECTIONS

RAYMOND C. BROWN
DIRECTOR

LARRY SOLOMON
ASSISTANT DIRECTOR

WILLIAM K. WILKEY
CHIEF, PRISONS DIVISION

AARON A. BROWN
PROJECT MONITOR

AMERICAN CORRECTIONAL ASSOCIATION

H.G. "GUS" MOELLER
PRESIDENT

ANTHONY P. TRAVISONO
EXECUTIVE DIRECTOR

ROBERT B. LEVINSON, PH.D.
PROJECT MANAGER

Resource Individuals

Aaron A. Brown
Correctional Program Manager
National Institute of Corrections
Washington, D.C.

Roy E. Gerard
(Assistant Director, Retired
Federal Bureau of Prisons)
Bluemont, Virginia

Robert B. Levinson, Ph.D.
(Deputy Assistant Director, Retired
Federal Bureau of Prisons)
American Correctional Association
College Park, Maryland

Craig T. Love, Ph.D.
Research Administrator
Southeast Region
Federal Correctional Institution
Butner, North Carolina

Charles M. Montgomery
Chief of Unit Management
Federal Bureau of Prisons
Washington, D.C.

W. Alan Smith, Ph.D.
Chief Psychologist
U.S. Penitentiary
Lewisburg, Pennsylvania

Herbert C. Quay, Ph.D.
Director, Program in Applied
  Social Sciences
Professor of Psychology and
  Pediatrics
University of Miami
Coral Gables, Florida

Project Staff

Robert B. Levinson, Ph.D.
Project Manager

Roberta L. Howard
Editor

Carol A. Sell
Staff Assistant

Martin J. Pociask
Art Director

Alonzo L. Winfield
Graphic Designer

Anne M. Burgess
Typographer

Annette Ryburn
Typographer

Graphics and typesetting by
ACA Services, Inc.

Contents

Foreword, ix
Preface, xi
Acknowledgments, xiii

Part I. User's Guide

Section 1. Introduction
Background, 3
In What Follows . . . , 5

Section 2. Inmate Groups
Group Labels: Old and New, 6
Group Characteristics, 6

Section 3. Implementation Processes
Making the Classification, 9
Implementing the Internal Management Approach, 14
Some General Principles, 17

Section 4. Advantages of the System
Administrative Options, 18
Utility of the System, 19

Section 5. Comparison With Other Classification Systems
Security Classification, 24
Custody Classification, 24
Salient Factor Scores, 26

Section 6. Implications for Correctional Practice
In-institution Practice, 28
System-wide Practice, 28
Conclusion, 29

Part II. Technical Data

Section 7. Development of the System
Rating Current Inmate Behavior: The Correctional Adjustment Checklist (CACL), 33

Analyzing Offender Records: The Life History Checklist (CALH), 35

Interrelationships Among Checklist Scales, 37

Section 8. Reliability and Validity
Reliability, 38

Validity, 38

Construct Validity of AIMS, 39

References, 51

Appendixes, 53

List of Exhibits

1. Correctional Adjustment Checklist (CACL): Sample Scoring, 12

2. Checklist for the Analysis of Life History Records of Adult Offenders (CALH): Sample Scoring, 13

3. Raw Score Form, Correctional Adjustment Checklist (CACL): Sample Scoring, 14

4. Raw Score Form, Life History Checklist (CALH): Sample Scoring, 15

5. Classification Profile for Adult Offenders: Sample Scoring, 16

List of Figures

1. The Classification Process, 3

2. Characteristic Group Behavior, 7

3. Differential Programming by Group Assignment, 19

4. Comparison of Security-level Implications, 24

5. Anticipated Relationship Between AIMS Groups and Institutional Adjustment, 38

6. Post-release Data: Total Sample, 44

7. Rearrest Data by Confinement vs. Non-confinement and Frequency of Occurrence, 46

8. Rearrest Data by Type of Crime and Frequency of Occurrence, 47

9. Violent vs. Nonviolent Rearrests, 48

LIST OF TABLES

1. Inmate Assaults on Staff in Five Penitentiaries: Comparison of Yearly Totals Pre- and Post-implementation of AIMS at Target Facility, 20

2. Inmate Assaults on Inmates in Five Penitentiaries: Comparison of Yearly Totals Pre- and Post-implementation of AIMS at Target Facility, 20

3. Cross-comparison of AIMS Groups and Bureau of Prisons Security Levels, 25

4. Cross-comparison of AIMS Groups and Bureau of Prisons Custody Levels, 25

5. Cross-comparison of AIMS Groups and U.S. Parole Commission Salient Factor Scores, 26

6. Congruency Coefficients for Correctional Adjustment Checklist (CACL), 34

7. Intercorrelations Among Correctional Adjustment Checklist (CACL) Scale Scores, 35

8. Congruency Coefficients for Life History Checklist (CALH), 36

9. Intercorrelations Among CACL and CALH Scales, 37

10. Significant Correlations Between CACL and CALH Scales and Other Variables, 39

11. Ethnic Distribution by AIMS Group (Two Institutions), 40

12. Age Distribution by AIMS Group (Two Institutions), 40

13. AIMS Group Means and SDs of IQ (Beta) Scores, 41

14. AIMS Group Means and SDs on MMPI Pd Scale, 41

15. AIMS Group Means and SDs on Megargee In-institution Work Performance Scale, 42

16. Unit-level (Minor) Disciplinary Infractions by AIMS Group (Two Institutions), 43

17. Institution-level (Major) Disciplinary Infractions by AIMS Group (Two Institutions), 43

Foreword

This manual brings together data on the development, validation, and utility of a behavioral classification system for adult offenders, a system that has been in operation for more than 15 years. During that time it has proved an effective tool for grouping inmates for both management and treatment purposes. The manual is intended to provide correctional administrators with the basic information needed to understand the nature of this system and make intelligent choices on its suitability for their own institutions.

Part I of the manual consists of six sections and is designed as a user's guide. Section I discusses how the Adult Internal Management System (AIMS) fits into the overall classification process and explains the distinctions between security level, custody level, and behavioral classification for determining housing assignments. Section 2 describes the inmate groups identified by AIMS and answers some general questions about the approach and its application. Section 3 explains the AIMS classification process and how to implement the approach in both existing and new institutions.

The utility of the system is discussed in Section 4, drawing on both research data and the experience of those who have used it. Section 5 compares the relationship between AIMS and three other approaches to classification: the security level and custody classification systems of the Federal Bureau of Prisons and the salient factor scores used by the U.S. Parole Commission. Section 6 explores implications for current correctional practices.

Part II of the manual describes the development of this behavioral classification system and offers technical data on its reliability and validity.

The Appendixes include the rating forms used by this system to classify inmates. Also included is the National Institute of Corrections' *Principles of Classification,* which specifies the essential elements of any classification process undertaken by correctional systems.

The American Correctional Association is pleased to be a part of this collaborative effort to bring together in a single document Dr. Herbert C. Quay's work on managing adult inmates. This publication represents the first attempt to present in a practical way all findings and experiences to date using this behavioral classification system. We hope it will receive wide reading leading to extensive implementation.

ANTHONY P. TRAVISONO
EXECUTIVE DIRECTOR
AMERICAN CORRECTIONAL ASSOCIATION
COLLEGE PARK, MARYLAND

Preface

Work on the internal behavioral classification system described in this document was done in the belief that offenders do not constitute a homogeneous group of people with the same behavior patterns, feelings, attitudes, and correctional needs. An overriding concern was to develop a scientifically sound approach for separating inmates into homogeneous subgroups that would have direct utility for more effective correctional rehabilitation and management.

Classification by definition involves separating inmates by their behavior and specific program needs. Devising efficient differential programs for each subgroup of offenders may remain a lofty ideal; effective management that creates a safe, secure, and humane correctional environment is not. Even if only the most limited number and types of rehabilitative programs are offered, the conscientious use of the Adult Internal Management System (AIMS) is still justified as a method to reduce inmate-to-staff and inmate-on-inmate violence, victimization, and extortion. The people who stand to benefit most from this system are the inmates themselves—particularly those who wish to pay their debt to society free from constant fear of, and intimidation by, a relatively small proportion of their peers.

No human creation, least of all one for dealing with our fellow man, is without probability of error. Applied psychometrics—the systematic measurement of behavioral characteristics—is an inexact technology. Consequently, any internal behavioral classification system certainly contains "error variance." Because AIMS must be implemented by humans, errors can occur ranging from careless and incompetent observation to incorrect addition of numbers. Clearly, the system is not immune from poor implementation, overly simplistic shortcuts, administrative mismanagement, or any other ill that a bureaucratic organization, public or private, can inflict on procedures for dealing with people. Therefore every user must remain alert to details and strive to reduce the probability of error.

One can only take consolation in the belief that not employing this system (or another capable of accomplishing the same ends) leads to a much less desirable situation than using it.

RAYMOND C. BROWN
DIRECTOR
NATIONAL INSTITUTE OF CORRECTIONS
WASHINGTON, D.C.

Acknowledgments

This manual incorporates data from a variety of sources. It supersedes the author's privately circulated paper entitled "The differential behavioral classification of the adult male offender: Interim results and procedures." The manual also includes data presented by the author at the annual meeting of the American Society of Criminology, 1973; the annual conventions of the American Psychological Association in 1981 and 1983; and the Canadian Psychological Association meeting in 1982. Where the work of others (published or unpublished) is cited, we hope that due credit has been given.

The vast majority of this work has been sponsored by the Bureau of Prisons, U. S. Department of Justice, and has involved a large number of Bureau personnel—from the Director to line correctional staff.

The work could not have been accomplished without the support and active collaboration of Director Norman A. Carlson, former Assistant Director Roy E. Gerard, former Deputy Assistant Director Robert B. Levinson, and former Research Director Howard L. Kitchener.

Immense help was provided by a number of former wardens, especially Charles Fenton and Jack Wise. Dr. W. Alan Smith, Chief Psychologist, U. S. Penitentiary, Lewisburg, Pennsylvania, became an expert in the practicalities of implementation of the system and supplied data on its validity. Dr. Craig T. Love, a former colleague and now Research Administrator for the Southeast Region of the Bureau of Prisons, played the major role in gathering and processing much of the data related to validity. Nick Howell, Research Analyst at the Federal Correctional Institution at Butner, North Carolina, performed invaluable computer analyses. Additional validity data were provided by Charles M. Montgomery, Chief of Unit Management, Bureau of Prisons, Washington, D.C.

The preparation of this manual has been greatly facilitated by the counsel of two of my collaborators, Roy Gerard and Bob Levinson. Valuable advice has also been provided by the National Institute of Corrections, in particular Aaron Brown and Bill Wilkey.

HERBERT C. QUAY, PH.D.
DIRECTOR, PROGRAM IN APPLIED SOCIAL SCIENCES
PROFESSOR OF PSYCHOLOGY AND PEDIATRICS
UNIVERSITY OF MIAMI
CORAL GABLES, FLORIDA
DECEMBER 1983

Part I. User's Guide

Section 1. Introduction

Section 2. Inmate Groups

Section 3. Implementation Processes

Section 4. Advantages of the System

Section 5. Comparison with Other Classification Systems

Section 6. Implications for Correctional Practice

1. Introduction

Every correctional system must be concerned about classifying its prisoners. Consequently, classification has been referred to as the key element in the administration of effective corrections. However, the term "classification" has taken on a surplus of connotations.

Recently an effort was made to help clarify the various definitions associated with the classification process (Levinson, 1982). As used in this publication, classification does *not* refer to levels of institutional security (see Stage I, Figure 1); the process by which a newly admitted offender is assigned to a particular institution is better labeled designation. Nor will this treatise be concerned with custody categories, which are properly defined as the degree of supervision required by a particular inmate (Stage III, Figure 1).

In this publication a method is discussed for placing inmates in housing—living—areas. This process frequently is not seen as an aspect of classification although it occurs in all prison facilities. Unfortunately, more often than not, vacant bedspace is the only critera for housing assignments. On occasion, attention may be paid to racial balance and/or equity in the amount of double (or triple) celling. Constitutionality and conditions of confinement issues frequently bring the courts onto the scene at this point.

Capitalizing on the fact that every incoming offender must be assigned a place to live, the following pages describe a more rational approach to sorting inmates at the *institutional* level. This procedure reduces conflict among inmates and minimizes management difficulties between prisoners and personnel. As a consequence, benefits accrue to all concerned.

Background

The assignment of prisoners to living quarters on the basis of some treatment and/or management objective has been tried in several institutions in a number of correctional systems. A frequent basis for such sorting has been the inmate's identified treatment need. For example, prisoners with drug addiction problems might be housed together to facilitate a therapeutic climate. Similarly, living areas might be established for alcoholics, sex offenders, the medically infirm, and geriatric or other special problem groups.

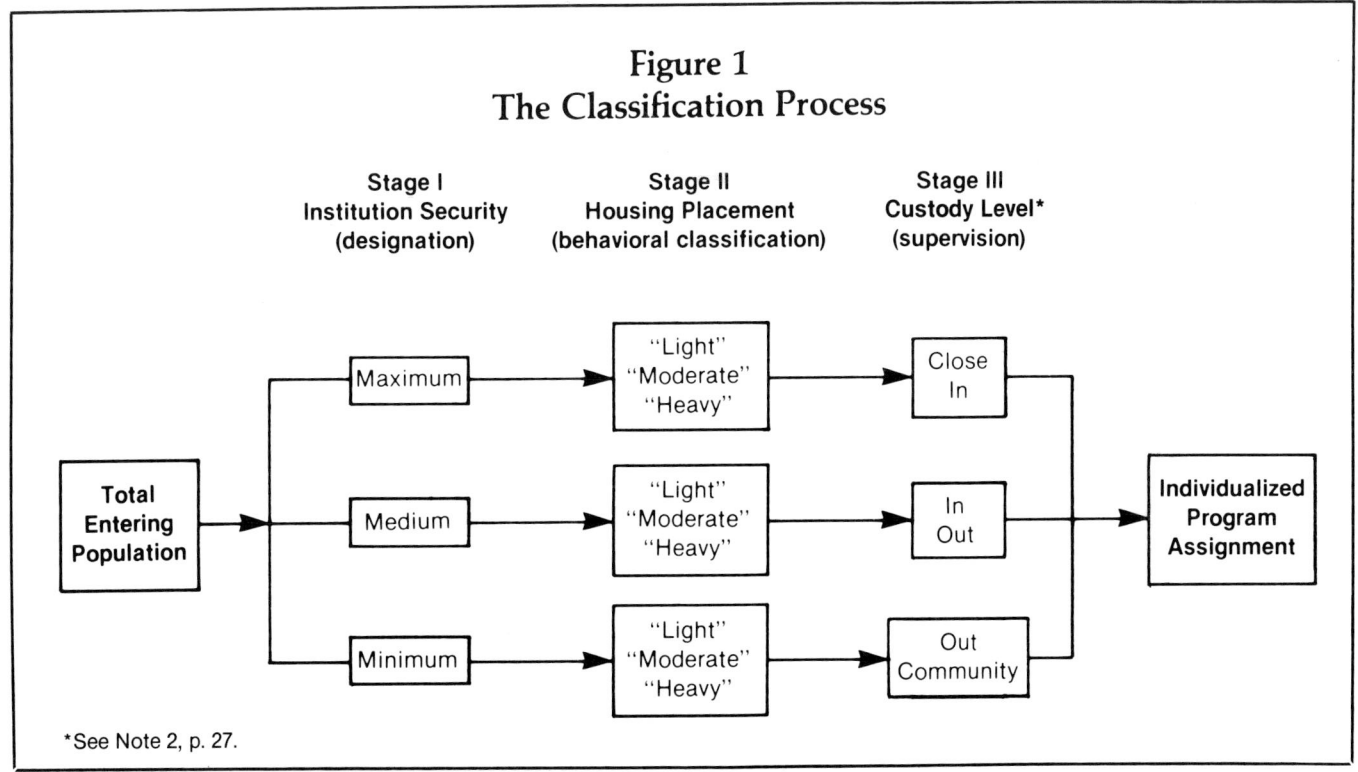

Figure 1
The Classification Process

*See Note 2, p. 27.

> It is not necessary to wait until inmate A assaults inmate Z before someone says, "Aha, A's a troublemaker!"

Inmates' work assignments have been used in some prisons to assign living quarters. Thus all kitchen workers (early risers) might live in the same area. Others might be grouped because they all work in prison industry or in the powerhouse or on the fire/emergency crew. This arrangement facilitates movement of prisoners to and from their work assignments and minimizes any daily disturbance of others.

Often, housing placement is based on separating behavior problems. Inmates who are frequently aggressive may be assigned to a particular wing or cell block. Alternatively, weaker, more victim-prone individuals may be housed closer to the officer's station for protective purposes. Usually such assignments are made after someone has been assaulted. It is possible, however, to replace this reactive stance with a more proactive program. That is, there are a variety of internal management classification procedures that, along with their other attributes, attempt to anticipate potential problems before they occur. Thus it is not necessary to wait until inmate A assaults inmate Z before someone says, "Aha, A's a troublemaker" or "It looks like Z needs to be protected."

Many of these "typology" systems were developed for use with juvenile or youthful offenders (Quay, 1965; Warren, 1969). More recently, typology systems have been developed for adult prisoners (e.g., Quay, 1974; Megargee & Bohn, 1979; Bureau of Prisons, 1979).

The concept underlying all of these efforts is the central issue in classification for inmate management:

identification
+
separation
=
reduced problems

This paradigm replicates the rationale for system-wide classification. In the latter, a systematic, objective assessment of all new admissions leads to a determination based on the individual's security requirements and supervisory needs. Those needing the tightest confinement are designated to maximum security institutions, while those requiring the least supervision are categorized as community custody inmates. Thus the escape-prone are sent to the penitentiaries and the nonviolent are given trusty status.

It is possible to conceive of an institution as a miniature correctional system. Although its range of new admissions is less broad than that received by the total department, nevertheless there are variations within its inmate population. Among an institution's prisoners there are the predators and their prey—the victimizers and the victim-prone. It makes the same good sense for the institution's management to separate these groups as it does for the correctional system's administrators to designate the repetitive violent individual to a prison different from the one to which the unsophisticated first offender is sent.

Although the degree of separation within an institution is not as great as can be achieved between institutions, much can still be accomplished. Not only can the "heavies" and "lights" live in different areas; it also may be possible (at least to some extent) to assign their program activities at different times. For example, the recreation yard might be scheduled for the "heavies" in the morning and the "lights" in the afternoon, with a reverse schedule for school or work assignments. While total separation cannot be expected, to the degree that some is accomplished opportunities for intimidation and assault will be reduced.

Further, the criteria on which this sorting-out process is based may contribute significantly to identifying which treatment programs will prove most cost-effective. For example, group therapy/counseling is not universally appropriate for all inmates—some may benefit, others may remain the same or even be made worse. There are no panaceas. Yet by exposing both appropriate and inappropriate prisoner/clients to any single treatment modality, an effective method may seem to offer no help since its good results with some inmates are obscured by its minimal effects on others.

The difficult trick is to determine what approach works best with whom and then make it available. By establishing treatment programs for homogeneous inmate groups, it becomes more feasible to ascertain the relative effectiveness of each regimen for specific types of prisoners. The smorgasbord can be replaced by a more targeted diet.

In What Follows...

This manual is devoted to exploring one approach to internal management. Its developer, Dr. Herbert C. Quay, has been working for more than two decades with the Federal Bureau of Prisons and a number of state correctional facilities. During that span of time his initial typology system for juvenile delinquents was expanded to include youthful offenders and was then reworked for adult prisoners.

Quay's approach is one of several in use (e.g., Megargee, 1979; Bureau of Prisons, 1979). A legitimate question to ask is: Why choose this approach over the others?

The National Institute of Corrections' publication *Prison Classification* (1981) lists fourteen "Principles of Classification," based on work reported by Solomon (1980). While designed to assess classification procedures of entire prison systems, these principles (Appendix 1) also have import for the internal management stage of a total approach. More directly relevant is the list of seven criteria for a good classification system published by Megargee (1977): the system should be complete, clear, reliable, valid, dynamic, economical, and have implications for treating offenders. Against both set of criteria, Quay's method of behavioral classification fares well.

It has been suggested that the most succinct way to express the purpose of an internal management classification system is: it separates the good guys from the bad guys when everybody is wearing a black hat. The sections that follow tell the "whys" and "hows" for doing just that.

An internal management classification system... separates the good guys from the bad guys when everybody is wearing a black hat.

2. Inmate Groups

The Adult Internal Management System (AIMS) classifies male offenders by sorting them into five categories (some of which may be combined to form a smaller number of groups). This permits individuals who require special management to be housed together. The process can reduce friction and violence among prisoners, facilitate institutional management, and make resource allocation more efficient.

At its simplest level, the system protects weaker inmates from stronger ones by separating potential victims from victimizers. It serves to insulate those within the prison who wish to conform and live in peace from those who do not. Most important, the method does not deny inmates any rights or privileges to which they would otherwise be entitled.

The heart of this internal management approach is a description of five offender groups and the process for placing individuals into one of these categories. In accomplishing this, AIMS relies on the inmates' *behavior*—past and present—rather than on characteristics such as age, race, marital status, type of offense leading to incarceration, etc. The system identifies potential problem prisoners early on, not waiting until after an incident has occurred.

Group Labels: Old and New

In earlier written materials and public presentations, five psychologically based labels were used to describe both the scales of the primary classification instruments used in this approach—the Correctional Adjustment Checklist and the Life History Checklist—and the five groups into which offenders can be placed. Those labels have now been replaced with numerical designations. What is here referred to as Scale I and Group I were previously labeled the Aggressive-Psychopathic (AP) scale and offender group; Scale II and Group II previously were the Manipulative (M) scale and inmate group; Scale III and Group III originally denoted the Situational (S) scale and prisoner group; Scale IV and Group IV had been referred to as Inadequate-Dependent (ID); and Scale V and Group V were previously labeled Neurotic-Anxious (NA).[1]

While it is hoped that these numerical designators will reduce any negative implications and overextended inferences, the very different behavior of the five offender groups soon becomes obvious to all, staff and inmates alike.

Group Characteristics

Group I consists of inmates who currently display (or have histories of) hostile, aggressive, and sometimes violent behavior. These individuals are resentful of rules and regulations and of staff efforts to control them. Many crave excitement; they become bored easily. Group I-type inmates have little concern for the feelings or welfare of others. They cause more than their share of serious disciplinary problems in institutions and are the individuals most likely to be involved in fighting, assaults, threats of bodily harm, extortion, destruction of property, and possession of weapons. Clearly these are the most troublesome prisoners and the ones most likely to be involved in major disturbances. Group I inmates have sometimes been referred to as aggressive or aggressive-psychopathic. They may be more simply conceived of as "heavies," "strongs," or "toughs." (See Figure 2, which summarizes each group's characteristic behaviors.)

Figure 2
Characteristic Behaviors by Group

I —————— Heavy —————— II		III — Moderate	IV —————— Light —————— V	
• Aggressive	• Sly	• Not excessively aggressive or dependent	• Dependent	• Constantly afraid
• Confrontational	• Not directly confrontational	• Reliable, cooperative	• Unreliable	• Anxious
• Easily bored	• Untrustworthy	• Industrious	• Passive	• Easily upset
• Hostile to authority	• Hostile to authority	• Do not see selves as criminals	• "Clinging"	• Seek protection
• High rate of disciplinary infractions	• Moderate-to-high rate of disciplinary infractions	• Low rate of disciplinary infractions	• Low-to-moderate rate of disciplinary infractions	• Moderate rate of disciplinary infractions
• Little concern for others	• "Con artists," manipulative	• Concern for others	• Self-absorbed	• Explosive under stress
• Victimizers	• Victimizers	• Avoid fights	• Easily victimized	• Easily victimized

Inmates in *Group II* usually do not have the same degree of outward aggressiveness as Group I prisoners. They are, however, hostile to authority and attempt to deal with others by "conning" or manipulative behavior; e. g., trying to play staff against one another, or setting up other prisoners for their own ends. Group II individuals may be the organizers of inmate gangs or illicit enterprises within the institution. They are generally seen by staff as being very untrustworthy and unreliable. Group II-type prisoners usually are not directly confrontational but instead tend to cause problems by operating behind the scenes. They have been referred to as "manipulators" or "con-artists" or "agitators."

Group III inmates are neither excessively aggressive nor dependent although the experience of being in prison may be demoralizing to them. They do not have extensive criminal histories nor do they see themselves as criminals. Group III prisoners have a low frequency of disciplinary problems and are rarely involved in assaults, fighting, threatening, or extortion.[2] Usually they avoid trouble and will fight only as a last resort. Group III individuals are generally the type of prisoner upon whom staff can rely. These inmates are often the backbone of prison industries. This group has been referred to as "situationals," "situational-normal," or "moderates" (since they are generally neither victims nor victimizers).

Offenders in *Group IV* are withdrawn, sluggish, unhappy, passive, and often give the impression of being "out of it." They are easily victimized by those in Groups I and II since they often are friendless and are seen as weak, indecisive, and submissive. Group IV inmates do not have a high rate of disciplinary problems; they are viewed by staff as demanding, whining, and clinging. Sometimes these individuals are described as "immature," "dependent," "weak sisters," or "lights."

Group V consists of prisoners who are constantly worried, anxious, afraid, jittery, easily upset, and unhappy. They appear sad, depressed, and tense—unable to relax. Inmates in Group V are also easily preyed upon by others. This group does not have a high rate of disciplinary infractions in the institution. When they are involved in misconduct, however, it is of a more serious nature since they tend to explode when they cannot handle additional stress. These individuals have sometimes been referred to as "neurotic-anxious" or "lights."

General Questions And Answers About The System

Q. With whom can the system be used?

A. The system was designed to be used with male inmates from age 18 upward. A similar system is available for male juveniles.[3] Neither of these is appropriate for female offenders.

The behavioral classification system can be used in any correctional facility that has at least two separate living units.

Q. *Where can it be used?*
A. It can be used in any correctional facility that has at least two separate living units.

Q. *Can it be used in jails?*
A. No and yes. The rapid turnover in the typical jail setting does not allow the collection of all the information necessary to classify unsentenced prisoners. However, this system can be useful for sentenced jail prisoners provided the necessary data are available.

Q. *Must all five groups be housed separately?*
A. No. Experience has shown that creating three housing groups—Group I & II (Heavies), Group III (Moderates), and Group IV & V (Lights)—is useful. The creation of even two such groups—Group I & II (Heavies) and a group containing all others—may be helpful. The ideal, of course, would be separate housing for each of the five groups.

Q. *What percentage of inmates will fall into the groups?*
A. This depends on the type of institution and the classification policies used to designate inmates to a particular institution. Inmates appropriately designated for a very secure institution might be distributed so that 35%-45% would be Heavies (in Groups I & II), 25%-30% Moderates (in Group III), and 25%-30% Lights (in Groups IV & V). A minimally secure, open institution whose inmates were appropriately designated would have 20%-25% Heavies, 40%-50% Moderates, and 30%-35% Lights.

Q. *How can I estimate percentages in the groups at my institution?*
A. The simplest way is to classify a random sample of the institution's population; e.g., classify all inmates whose number ends in any two digits, say "3" and "8." Such a sample should be about 20% of the population or 100 inmates, whichever is smaller.

Notes

1. In earlier drafts of this manuscript Group III was listed as Inadequate-Dependent, Group IV as Neurotic-Anxious, and Group V as Situational.

2. Group III may include some highly sophisticated criminals (such as leaders of organized crime) who often avoid frequent contact with the courts. The classification system separates them from their "enforcers."

3. The classification system for juveniles is described in H.C. Quay and L.B. Parsons, *The Differential Behavioral Classification of the Juvenile Offender*, which was published by the Federal Bureau of Prisons; a revision of this system is currently in process.

3. Implementation Processes

Making The Classification

The classification process—obtaining information about the inmate, developing the inmate's profile, and assigning the inmate to a group—involves nine basic steps. They are all essential and must be undertaken in sequence.

Obtaining Information About The Inmate

Information concerning the behavior of the inmate during the admission and orientation (A&O) period, as rated by correctional staff, is combined with data regarding the inmate's past behavior. The historical material is obtained by a case manager or caseworker, based on a rating made from information contained in the presentence report (or equivalent).

Step 1. At the end of the A&O period, one or more of the correctional officers regularly assigned to the A&O unit completes the Correctional Adjustment Checklist (CACL)—see Appendix 2. Judgments about the items on the CACL are based on the inmate's behavior (adjustment) during the A&O period.

Step 2. After reading the presentence report (or its equivalent), interviewing the prisoner, and using any other records available, the case manager (or caseworker) completes the Checklist for the Analysis of Life History Records of Adult Offenders (CALH)—see Appendix 3.

Questions And Answers About Obtaining Information

Q. *Is an A&O unit necessary to classify new inmates?*

A. Ideally, yes, unless classification into one of the groups is made at a central reception and diagnostic facility. Departments of corrections that employ a centralized reception/diagnostic approach can conduct these classification procedures during the period prior to designation to an appropriate institution.

Q. *How long an A&O period is required?*

A. The A&O staff must have an opportunity to observe the behavior of the inmate being classified before completing the Adjustment Checklist. A three- to four-week observation period is ideal but ten days to two weeks may suffice.

Q. *What if the institution does not have an A&O unit?*

A. If absolutely necessary, an initial classification can be made using only the Life History Checklist—based solely on the presentence report (or its equivalent). After an opportunity to observe the inmate, the Adjustment Checklist can be completed and the prisoner reclassified using both forms.

Q. *Suppose the institution does not receive presentence reports (or some equivalent)?*

A. In that case the initial classification *can* be made using only the Adjustment Checklist. When a social history has been obtained through interviewing, the Life History Checklist can be completed and a reclassification undertaken using both forms.

Q. *What if the institution does not have an A&O unit and does not obtain presentence reports?*

A. A life history interview can be conducted; then the Life History Checklist is completed and an initial classification made. After there has been an opportunity to observe the inmate, the Adjust-

> Two checklists are scored and the results combined to make the classification.... The highest Final Score determines which of the five groups the inmate is assigned to.

ment Checklist can be completed and the individual reclassified using both forms.

USING THE INFORMATION TO OBTAIN AN INMATE'S PROFILE

Both the Correctional Adjustment (CACL) and the Life History (CALH) checklists contain items that reflect behavior and life events associated with the five AIMS groups. The two checklists are scored and the results combined to make the classification.

Step 3. The inmate's adjustment is scored for four groups (I, II, IV, V) according to the CACL scoring form (Appendix 4).

Step 4. The inmate's life history is scored for three groups (I, III, IV) according to the CALH scoring form (Appendix 5).

Step 5. The inmate's Total Score for each group on the two checklists is entered in the appropriate Raw Score column of the Classification Profile Sheet (Appendix 6).

Step 6. The Raw Scores from both checklists are converted to T-scores.[1] (See Appendixes 7 and 8 for the appropriate conversion tables.)

Step 6a. If Adjustment Checklist ratings have been obtained from two correctional officers, the two T-scores for each adjustment scale are added together and each sum is divided by 2.

Step 7. The T-scores obtained for Scales II and V of the Adjustment Checklist and Scale III of the Life History Checklist represent the Final T-scores for those three scales. To obtain the Final T-scores for Scale I, the CACL T-score for Scale I is added to the CALH T-score for Scale I and the sum is divided by 2; the same process is used to determine the Final T-score for Scale IV.

ASSIGNING THE INMATE TO A GROUP

The highest Final Score determines which of the five groups the inmate is assigned to. The number of available separate living units determines whether the AIMS groups must be combined.

Step 8. The highest Final Score determines to which of the five groups the inmate is assigned.

Step 9. If five separate living units are available, prisoners are placed in the unit in which their group is housed.

Step 9a. If four separate living units are available, then Groups I & II are combined; the remaining groups are each housed separately.

Step 9b. If three separate living units are available, then Groups I & II are combined as are Groups IV & V, and Group III is housed separately.

Step 9c. If only two separate living units are available, Groups I & II are housed together as are Groups III, IV, & V.

AN EXAMPLE OF THE CLASSIFICATION PROCESS

The following discussion illustrates how an inmate might be classified on the basis of prior life history and behavior during the A&O period.

Inmate X, a 25-year-old, has been sentenced to 25 years for bank robbery. He was first arrested at age 15 for mugging, after having been expelled from school for hitting a teacher. Following additional arrests, he served a previous sentence of three years in a state prison for strong-arm robbery. X now presents himself with considerable bravado and openly expresses an "every man for himself" attitude, blaming others for his problems. He admits to having few friends. He has never held any one job for more than three consecutive months.

During the two-week admission and orientation period, inmate X presented a "tough guy" image and was involved in extorting commissary goods from other prisoners. He was constantly swearing at and threatening other inmates and talked aggressively to staff as well. X was openly defiant of institution rules and on one occasion appeared to deliberately interfere with the count. He gravitated toward associating with inmates who had prior prison experience.

Exhibit 1 represents a completed Adjustment Checklist rating for inmate X and Exhibit 2 a completed Life History Checklist rating. His scale scores are shown in Exhibits 3 and 4; his classification profile in Exhibit 5. In this illustration inmate X obviously is a Heavy (Group I) and is so classified.

Questions And Answers About Assigning Inmates To Groups

Q. *What happens in those few instances when two (or more) final scores are the same?*

A. There are three tie-breaking levels: (1) rescore all forms and check all calculations; (2) use the guidelines at the bottom of the Classification Profile form (Appendix 6); or (3) assign the inmate on the basis of a staff consensus as to the group in which the inmate is likely to fit best, noting this information on the Classification Profile form.

Q. *How can I be sure an inmate's classification is correct?*

A. You can't, since no classification, custody, or parole prediction procedure is perfectly accurate. Careful ratings by correctional officers, counselors, and caseworkers are your best guarantee. The purpose of the Adjustment and Life History ratings is to make certain that the classifications are empirically based, not arbitrary or just "seat of the pants" decisions.

Q. *What about errors and misclassifications?*

A. It will sometimes appear, based on the offender's behavior, that an inmate is in the "wrong" group. When this occurs, *first,* check to be certain that errors were not made in scoring either checklist, or in adding the scores, or in obtaining the T-scores. If no error occurred, then it is most likely that a true picture of the inmate's adjustment was not obtained during the A&O period. Therefore, *second,* a new Adjustment Checklist should be completed. This new CACL can be used in conjunction with the old Life History Checklist to arrive at the individual's group classification (if no new case history information has been received). *Third,* if new history material is available to the caseworker, a new Life History Checklist can be completed as well and then the re-evaluation obtained. If all these procedures yield no change in the classification, the inmate remains in the current group assignment.

Q. *How can a manager deal with severe overcrowding in one living unit and less crowding in another?*

A. Five adjustment methods can be used to permit some flexibility in how inmates are assigned to groups, thus enabling managers to deal with such issues as availability of bed space in a particular unit or maintaining racial balance. *First,* newly admitted Moderates can be used to fill vacancies in either Heavy or Light units. *Second,* the number of housing units assigned to each group can be altered, or, *third,* some compatible smaller groups can be combined. *Fourth,* as discussed above, tied scores permit some flexibility; in addition, scores that are not actually tied but are very nearly the same (one or two points difference in T-scores) can be handled as if they were tied. A *fifth* method is to adjust the criteria for assigning inmates to certain groups. For example, assume an institution has three housing units, one for Heavies, one for Moderates, and the third for Lights. If the number of Heavies is exceeding the available bedspace, the assignment rule can be changed *temporarily* so that either the Group I or Group II score for a new admission must be, say, at least five points higher than any other score in order for that inmate to be assigned to the Heavy unit.

Q. *What are the most serious errors in assigning prisoners to living units?*

A. The most serious mistake is to place a Group IV or V inmate (Light) into a Group I or II unit (Heavy). Heavy inmates in Light units also must be avoided. Lights or Heavies misplaced into the Moderate living area are less damaging since the Moderates are the most stable and can probably deal better with inmates misclassified into their units.

> **No classification, custody, or parole prediction procedure is perfectly accurate. Careful ratings by correctional officers, counselors, and caseworkers are the best guarantee.**

Exhibit 1
Correctional Adjustment Checklist (CACL): Sample Scoring

Name and number of inmate "X"
Name of person completing this checklist David Smith
Your position Correctional Officer   Date completed 7/2/84

Instructions: Please indicate which of the following behaviors this inmate exhibits. If the behavior describes the inmate, circle "1." If it does not, circle "0." *Please complete every item.*

0	1	1. Worried, anxious
0	1	2. Tries, but cannot seem to follow directions
0	1	3. Tense, unable to relax
0	1	4. Socially withdrawn
0	1	5. Continually asks for help from staff
0	①	6. Gets along with the hoods
0	1	7. Seems to take no pleasure in anything
0	1	8. Jittery, jumpy; seems afraid
0	1	9. Uses leisure time to cause trouble
0	①	10. Continually uses profane language; curses and swears
0	1	11. Easily upset
0	1	12. Sluggish and drowsy
0	1	13. Cannot be trusted at all
0	1	14. Moody, brooding
0	1	15. Needs constant supervision
0	①	16. Victimizes weaker inmates
0	1	17. Seems dull and unintelligent
0	1	18. Is an agitator about race
0	1	19. Continually tries to con staff
0	1	20. Impulsive; unpredictable
0	1	21. Afraid of other inmates
0	1	22. Seems to seek excitement
0	1	23. Never seems happy
0	1	24. Doesn't trust staff
0	1	25. Passive; easily led
0	①	26. Talks aggressively to other inmates
0	1	27. Accepts no blame for any of his troubles
0	1	28. Continually complains; accuses staff of unfairness
0	1	29. Daydreams; seems to be mentally off in space
0	①	30. Talks aggressively to staff
0	1	31. Has a quick temper
0	1	32. Obviously holds grudges; seeks to "get even"
0	1	33. Inattentive; seems preoccupied
0	1	34. Attempts to play staff against one another
0	1	35. Passively resistant; has to be forced to participate
0	1	36. Tries to form a clique
0	①	37. Openly defies regulations and rules
0	1	38. Often sad and depressed
0	1	39. Stirs up trouble among inmates
0	1	40. Aids or abets others in breaking the rules
0	1	41. Considers himself unjustly confined

Source: Herbert C. Quay, Ph.D.

Exhibit 2
Checklist for the Analysis of Life History Records of Adult Offenders (CALH): Sample Scoring

Name and number of inmate __"X"__
Name of person completing this checklist __Jane Jones__
Your position __Caseworker__   Date completed __7/5/84__

Instructions: Place a checkmark before each behavior trait that describes this inmate's life history.

✓	1. Has few, if any, friends
	2. Thrill-seeking
	3. Preoccupied; "dreamy"
	4. Uncontrollable as a child
	5. Has expressed guilt over offense
	6. Expresses need for self-improvement
	7. Socially withdrawn
	8. Weak, indecisive, easily led
✓	9. Previous local, state, or federal incarceration
	10. Tough, defiant
✓	11. Irregular work history (if not a student)
	12. Noted not to be responsive to counseling
	13. Gives impression of ineptness, incompetence in managing everyday problems in living
	14. Supported wife and children
	15. Claims offense was motivated by family problems
	16. Close ties with criminal elements
	17. Depressed, morose
✓	18. Physically aggressive (strong arm, assault, reckless homicide, attempted murder, mugging, etc.)
	19. Apprehension likely due to "stupid" behavior on the part of the offender
	20. Single marriage
	21. Expresses feelings of inadequacy, worthlessness
✓	22. Difficulties in the public schools
	23. Suffered financial reverses prior to commission of offense for which incarcerated
	24. Passive, submissive
✓	25. Bravado, braggart
✓	26. Guiltless; blames others
✓	27. Expresses lack of concern for others

Source: Herbert C. Quay, Ph.D.

Q. *Can inmates change their classification by "good behavior"?*

A. No. But they may become *less* aggressive, *less* dependent, *less* manipulative, etc. When such improvement occurs, prisoners can be promoted to less restrictive custody or transfers can be considered—for example, to a special program or to an industries unit. Such changes, of course, are on a round-trip ticket; inmates who don't work out well are returned to their original group's housing area. Similarly, a Group V individual may get a disciplinary report and be placed in segregation. When released from segregation, the inmate returns to Group V housing, possibly in a more restrictive custody category.

Q. *Does "labeling" inmates cause them to "act like their labels"?*

A. There is no evidence that it does. In order to get "labeled," an offender not only must have a history of the behavior associated with a particular group but must have shown that type of behavior during the A&O period. A prisoner who shows none of the characteristics of Groups I, II, IV, or V will be in Group III by exclusion. Staff should be made aware through formal training sessions that there will be "good" and "bad" prisoners in all the AIMS groups; moreover, inmates can change for the better, no matter what their group. It is important to stress that group identity can not be used to deny privileges for which the prisoner would otherwise be eligible.

Q. *Will this approach withstand legal challenge?*

A. There has been no serious challenge or court ruling criticizing the system during its use by the Federal Prison System. On occasion, inmates have questioned the point scoring on a particular item; i.e., have challenged the accuracy of information in their criminal history record.

Exhibit 3
Raw Score Form, Correctional Adjustment Checklist (CACL): Sample Scoring

Name and number of inmate __"X"__
Name of person completing this checklist __John Doe__
Your position __Counselor__ Date completed __7/2/84__

Instructions: For each "1" circled on the Correctional Adjustment Checklist, place a checkmark on the line corresponding to the item number. Add the checkmarks to obtain the Raw Score for each group.

Group			
I	II	IV	V
			1. ___
		2. ___	3. ___
		4. ___	5. ___
6. ✓		7. ___	8. ___
9. ___			
10. ✓			11. ___
		12. ___	
13. ___		14. ___	
15. ___			
16. ✓		17. ___	
18. ___	19. ___		
20. ___			21. ___
22. ___		23. ___	
	24. ___	25. ___	
26. ✓			
27. ___	28. ___	29. ___	
30. ✓			
31. ___			
32. ___		33. ___	
	34. ___	35. ___	
36. ___			
37. ✓			38. ___
39. ___			
40. ___	41. ___		
Total (Raw Score) 6	0	0	0

Implementing The Internal Management Approach

The internal behavioral classification system can be implemented under two separate conditions: reorganizing an existing facility and opening a new institution. Each circumstance presents problems and opportunities.

Reorganizing An Existing Institution

Orientation and training. All inmates and staff, including staff at all levels, must be informed about what is going to take place and why. It should be emphasized to personnel and prisoners alike that both groups will benefit—that the proper use of this new classification system will result in an institution that is safer for inmates and easier for staff to operate. The differences among the offender groups should be explained to all in simple, nonderogatory language.

Those staff who will be involved in making the group classifications should be trained and made familiar with the Adjustment and Life History checklists. Making accurate ratings should be emphasized. Appropriate classification—and thus how well the total system functions—depends on being conscientious. Personnel completing the forms and managers using this information for decision-making purposes should be knowledgeable about, and diligent in following, written policy and procedures.

Making the initial classification. If an existing institution is to be reorganized, all inmates will have to be reclassified. The staff members who best know each prisoner should complete the Adjustment Checklist; the inmate's caseworker or case manager should complete the Life History Checklist.

Next, an A&O unit should be initiated (if one is not already functioning) and the observation period made operational.

Moving into assigned housing. After the appropriate group for each inmate is identified, a large number of prisoners will have to move from their present housing to the "correct" living area. This can be accomplished in a mass movement (for instance, during a weekend) or it can be phased-in over time. If the latter alternative is chosen, the phase-in process should not be dragged out over a long period; 60 to 90 days should offer enough time. Also, it is most important that the Heavies— Groups I & II—be the first ones relocated in the process.

Opening A New Institution

When the Adult Internal Management System is to be used in a new facility, an opportunity exists to implement this approach under conditions that should be close to ideal. Because staff understanding and commitment to the new system is crucial, adequate time can be spent in employee orientation and training, and personnel can be specially selected to operate the A&O unit. Differential staffing of some units can also be planned (see Section 4).

If planning decisions are made early enough, the facility should be designed around unit management (Levinson & Gerard, 1972) and behavioral classification. As described in *Design Guide for Secure Adult Correctional Facilities*, developed by the American Correctional Association (1983) and the National Institute of Corrections, this approach has yielded positive results.

Questions And Answers On Implementation

Q. In an on-going institution, how are all the on-board inmates evaluated for

---

Exhibit 4
Raw Score Form, Life History Checklist (CALH): Sample Scoring

Name and number of inmate: "X"
Name of person completing this checklist: Jane Jones
Your position: Caseworker   Date completed: 7/5/84

Instructions: For each item checked on the Checklist for the Analysis of Life History Records of Adult Offenders, place a checkmark on the line corresponding to the item number. Add the checkmarks to obtain the Raw Score for each group.

Group I	Group III	Group IV
		1. ✓
2. ___		3. ___
4. ___		
	5. ___	
	6. ___	
		7. ___
		8. ___
9. ✓		
10. ___		
11. ✓		
12. ___		13. ___
	14. ___	
	15. ___	
16. ___		17. ___
18. ✓		19. ___
	20. ___	
		21. ___
22. ✓	23. ___	
		24. ___
25. ✓		
26. ✓		
27. ✓		
Total (Raw Score): 7	**0**	**1**

Exhibit 5
Classification Profile for Adult Offenders: Sample Scoring

Name and number of inmate "X"
Name of person completing this profile Jane Jones
Your position Case worker   Date completed 7/12/84

	Scale	Raw score	T-score
1. Correctional Adjustment Checklist (CACL)	I	6	60
	II	0	44
	IV	0	40
	V	0	39
Checklist for the Analysis of Life History Records (CALH)	I	7	64
	III	0	39
	IV	1	47

2. Combined Scores

Scale	CACL T-score		CALH T-score		Final T-score
I	60	+	64	÷ 2 =	62
II	44			=	44
III			39	=	39
IV	40	+	47	÷ 2 =	43.5
V	39			=	39

3. Assignment   ✓ Group I   ___ Group III   ___ Group IV
                ___ Group II   ___ Group V

---

placement into the AIMS groups?

A. Staff in an on-going facility are already familiar with their inmates. On a one-time basis, the most knowledgeable staff members perform the ratings; e.g., the prisoner's present caseworker completes the Life History Checklist (using all available records) and the day and/or evening correctional officer (or officers) complete the Correctional Adjustment Checklist(s). These activities are performed following staff's exposure to "hands-on" training sessions.

Q. *How do you classify inmates in long-term segregation status?*

A. The procedures used are the same as those used with regular inmates. The classification takes place when these individuals are ready to *come off* segregation status.

Q. *How are transfers handled?*

A. Transfers from other facilities within the system are handled as if they were new admissions. That is, they receive an orientation to their new facility in the A&O unit and, based on their social history and behavior rating forms, are placed in the appropriate living quarters.

Q. *Do new forms have to be completed for individuals who return to the institution after being released or transferred out?*

A. Generally, completing new forms would be desirable; new circumstances may have occurred during the interim that could affect the scoring. However, to avoid unnecessary work, a facility could adopt a procedural rule so that, say, only those who have been away from the facility for more than six months have to go through the total classification procedure.

SOME GENERAL PRINCIPLES

MANAGEMENT'S COMMITMENT

The importance of commitment by top-level administrative staff cannot be overstated. If the chief executive officer does not understand and actively support it, the Adult Internal Management System will fail. Conveying the attitude that the new approach is "nonsense" or that one individual alone can do it better will also undermine the effort. Adapting to change is difficult enough without these added burdens.

EQUAL PROGRAM OPPORTUNITY

Classification and separate housing for the identified groups should not deny inmates the right to participate in any of the institution's custody levels or program activities. In addition to being housed differentially, prisoners should participate in as many group activities as possible (e.g., education, recreation, meals) with other members of their own group. Contact between Light and Heavy inmates in particular should be minimized through careful scheduling.

NOTES

1. A T-score is a way of using statistical methods to make different scales equal. Looking at the conversion scores in Appendix 7, for example, it can be seen that a raw score of 2 on Scale II and a raw score of 5 on Scale IV both have T-scores of 59; thus, a score of 5 on longer Scale IV equals a score of 2 on short Scale II.

> **The importance of commitment by top-level administrative staff cannot be overstated. If the chief executive officer does not understand and actively support it, the new approach will fail.**

4. Advantages of the System

> Staff may feel more comfortable working with certain inmates than with others. Where practical, allowing personnel a choice about the group with whom they will work can be effective.

Administrative Options

Once inmates who share behavioral characteristics are grouped together a variety of positive considerations becomes possible.

Unit Management

Use of this internal behavioral classification system provides a vehicle for efficient unit management (Levinson & Gerard, 1972). By subdividing an institution's total population into smaller components—usually organized around housing areas—and identifying staff members with offenders assigned to each unit, better staff/inmate relationships develop. This approach has led to fewer management problems and inter-inmate conflicts. Additionally, programs can be targeted for the different prisoner groups, thereby enhancing the likelihood of these activities having a significant positive impact.

While this guide argues for organizing units around behavioral types, other approaches have also been effective; e.g., chemical abuse units (drug, alcohol), mental health units, geriatric units, prison industry units.

Staff Allocation

Since Groups I and II present the greatest management problems, proportionately more correctional staff may be assigned to them. Group III should present the fewest problems; therefore proportionately fewer correctional staff may be needed in their living area. Groups IV and V may need a greater proportion of program staff. Thus, more efficient use is made of available staff resources.

Differential Staff Assignment

Staff, both line officers and caseworkers, may feel more comfortable working with certain inmates than with others. Where practical, allowing personnel a choice about the group with whom they will work can be most effective, provided their selections are based on a good understanding of the characteristics of the different groups.

Administrators using this management strategy should take staff characteristics into consideration as well. This will result in less stressed, more effective personnel. For example, the no-nonsense, by-the-book type of staff member is likely to interact more appropriately with the Heavy inmates (Groups I & II), while personnel who favor the "let's-sit-down-and-talk-about-your-problem" approach will probably relate more effectively with Light prisoners (Groups IV & V).

Differential Programming

As shown in Figure 3, clustering inmates by behavioral characteristics allows staff to plan and offer more appropriate programs for each of the groups. Such differential programming is frequently a matter of how an individual is approached rather than large differences in the subject matter itself.

For example, short-term goals and immediate, tangible rewards are most effective for Groups I & II; individual sports and nonrepetitive work are most appropriate, as is a programmed learning approach to education and vocational training. In contrast, team sports and repetitive-type work are better choices for Groups IV & V; individuals in these groups also respond to counseling sessions and other types of verbal interaction. Thus the typical classroom lecture approach, with individualized instruction if necessary, will be more productive with these offenders. The program guide for Group III is "do no harm"; they

Figure 3
Differential Programming by Group Assignment

	Education	Work	Counseling	Staff Approach
Heavy (Groups I & II)	• Individualized • Programmed learning	• Non-repetitive • Short-term goals • Individual goals	• Individualized (behavioral contracts)	• By-the-book • No-nonsense
Moderate (Group III)	• Classroom lecture plus research assignments	• High level of supervised responsibility	• Group and individual (problem orientation)	• "Hands off" • Direct only as needed
Light (Groups IV & V)	• Classroom lecture plus individual tutoring	• Repetitive • Team-oriented goals	• Group and individual (personal orientation)	• Highly verbal • Supportive

will function best if given a high level of supervised responsibilities.

UTILITY OF THE SYSTEM

The Adult Internal Management System for classifying prisoners has demonstrated several different types of validity; these are discussed in detail in Part II of this manual. We turn now to the question of utility and ask: How has implementation of this internal management system facilitated the attainment of desirable correctional objectives?

It must be recognized at the outset that hard data on the effectiveness of correctional interventions are difficult to come by. Prisons do not easily lend themselves to classical experimental-vs.-control studies. In most correctional settings, it is next to impossible to hold all other factors constant while one manipulates the variable of interest. Absent the definitive experiment, we must rely on bits and pieces of data and on the informed, considered opinions of experienced correctional administrators.

Reduction of Inmate Violence

A large maximum security penitentiary implemented AIMS by classifying all its inmates and providing separate housing for three groups—Heavies, Moderates, Lights. In part, this implementation—and, concomitantly, the initiation of unit management—was motivated by an existing high level of inmate violence (Smith & Fenton, 1978).

The data of interest here are frequency of inmate assaults on both staff and other prisoners. The target institution, which had the largest population, was compared with four other penitentiaries for the year prior to introduction of the internal management system and during the four years following its implementation (Tables 1 and 2). Because the prisons were of different sizes, the average size of the smallest institution during the years in which data were collected was taken as a base (100)—see column 2, Tables 1 and 2—and the size of the other facilities was expressed as a multiple of that base. Thus the target institution was slightly more than two-and-one-half times larger than the smallest (facility P in the tables).

Inmate-on-staff violence. The percentages at the bottom of Table 1 compare the actual number of assaults on staff in the target institution with the number that would have been expected (based on the facility's size and the total number occurring in all five institutions). It was anticipated that the target institution would have 27% (255/946) of these incidents each year, while the other penitentiaries combined were expected to have the remaining 73% (691/946).

In the year prior to implementing AIMS, the target institution suffered 33% of the total number of assaults on staff occurring in all five facilities, com-

> The assault rate on staff at the target facility was... well below half the rate expected.

Table 1
Inmate Assaults on Staff in Five Penitentiaries:
Comparison of Yearly Totals Pre- and Post-implementation of AIMS at Target Facility

Penitentiary	Population base	Pre-AIMS	Post-AIMS			
		Year 0	Year 1	Year 2	Year 3	Year 4
P	(100)	3	10	16	15	12
Q	(182)	6	16	18	15	21
R	(202)	9	14	17	15	10
S	(207)	4	14	12	24	19
Target	(255)	11	3	15	5	9
	(946)	33	57	78	74	71
% of assaults at target facility						
Expected		27%	27%	27%	27%	27%
Actual		33%	5%	20%	7%	13%

pared to the 27% it was expected to have. Although the anticipated value for the other four institutions was 73% of this total, they actually had 67%. These differences, however, were nowhere near statistically significant; i.e., none of these prisons deviated significantly at first from their statistically anticipated number of inmate-on-staff assaults.[1]

The statistics for the first year following implementation of AIMS were notable: While the number of assaults on staff in all five institutions rose above the total for the previous year, the number

Table 2
Inmate Assaults on Inmates in Five Penitentiaries:
Comparison of Yearly Totals Pre- and Post-implementation of AIMS at Target Facility

Penitentiary	Population base	Pre-AIMS	Post-AIMS			
		Year 0	Year 1	Year 2	Year 3	Year 4
P	(100)	8	18	18	21	17
Q	(182)	36	19	30	25	20
R	(202)	17	32	50	30	24
S	(207)	27	22	19	23	33
Target	(255)	19	9	31	17	13
	(946)	107	100	148	116	107
% of assaults at target facility						
Expected		27%	27%	27%	27%	27%
Actual		18%	9%	21%	15%	12%

of assaults in the target institution dropped considerably—from 11 to 3. During that year the target facility experienced only 5% of the total vs. the 27% expected—statistically a highly significant difference.[2] Post-year 2 saw a continued increase in assaults in all institutions, the target facility included. However, the number of assaults on staff at the target institution—15, or 20% of the total number—again remained statistically significantly below expectations.[3] In the third post-year, while total assaults remained at a high level, the target institution's rate dropped to only 7% of the total—5 of 74; the actual-vs.-expected difference is highly statistically significant.[4] In the last year for which data were collected, the target institution continued at a level statistically significantly below expectations—13% actual vs. 27% expected.[5]

Thus, in each of the four years following implementation of this behavioral classification system, the target facility experienced fewer inmate assaults on staff than would have been expected on the basis of its size (when compared to facilities serving similar types of prisoners). For the total four-year period following introduction of AIMS, the assault rate on staff at the target penitentiary was 11.4% of the total (32/280), well below half the rate expected.

Inmate-on-inmate violence. Table 2 provides data regarding inmate assaults on other prisoners. In the pre-implementation year, the target facility had significantly fewer assaults—18% of the total—than might be expected based on relative population sizes.[6] In the first post-year there was a 50% drop at the target institution, which declined to 9% of the total, statistically a highly significant departure from the expected number.[7]

In the second year post-implementation, there was a 48% increase in prisoner assaults on other inmates in the five penitentiaries; the target institution experienced a three-fold increase. Nevertheless, the number of assaults remained slightly, although not significantly, below expectations for the target facility.[8] In both the third and fourth post-implementation years, inmate-on-inmate violence in the target institution was statistically significantly below expectations.[9] For the total four-year post-AIMS period, the inmate-on-inmate assault rate at the target penitentiary was 14.8% of the total (70/471), or slightly above half the rate expected.

Summary. Overall, use of AIMS was associated (in all years except one) with a statistically significant reduction in both types of violence—inmate-on-inmate and inmate-to-staff. In only two instances did the actual amount of post-implementation assaults exceed that of the pre-initiation year, despite overall trends toward increasing violence in similar institutions during that same time period.[10]

There are, of course, many variables associated with inmate violence, and we can only assume that these operated randomly across all five facilities. At the same time there is no immediately apparent plausible alternative to explain the consistent reduction of inmate violence below the expected rate in the penitentiary that instituted AIMS.[11]

REDUCTION OF INMATE MISCONDUCT

Further information on this behavioral classification approach and inmate institutional adjustment has been provided by data from a state correctional system. Auffrey (1978) compared prison disciplinary records pre- and post-implementation of AIMS in a medium security state institution. He reported (p.19):

> For major misconduct, minor misconduct and summary actions, the average for four months post [implementation] is substantially lower, although not statistically significant. Since the magnitude of misconducts, fighting tickets, etc., has always been low at MCF, the impact of the system may be difficult to gauge using these variables.

> . . . the inmate-on-inmate assault rate was . . . (approximately) half the rate expected.

> "There are a number of management devices which are used for control, and I would be loathe to part with any of them, but the foundation (at this institution) is the division by personality groupings."

Auffrey's data (p.20) also show that the living unit that housed Group III (Moderate) inmates had a substantial (61%) and statistically significant reduction in major misconducts (p = .05) compared with the prior period when it housed a much more heterogeneous group. The unit housing combined Groups IV & V experienced a 40% reduction in major disciplinary reports; this difference, however, failed to reach statistical significance. Auffrey concluded (p.20): "The increased manageability and more favorable resident adjustment on these units is seen as a direct result of the classification procedures and the differing staff philosophy which follows a change in the unit populations."

Grievances filed by inmates were also studied (Auffrey, 1978, p.19): "The number of resident grievances has declined substantially since the institution of the system. This change is statistically significant at the .05 level."

Views from Administrators

One of the first institutions to use this internal management system was a facility for younger offenders with relatively long sentences. The warden of that prison summed up his experience as follows:

> The prime need at this institution is control. Control not only in the correctional sense of preventing escapes and serious acting-out behavior, but also in the conventional business sense of accounting for and managing resources, human and materiel. The physical plant does not lend itself to these purposes. It is designed as a school with a fence around it and was intended for short-term juveniles rather than long-term adults.
>
> By dividing the population into units based on their personality characteristics, we have been able to establish the controls which are essential. The large group interaction found in most institutions, which is based on organization or functioning of predatory gangs, is virtually non-existent. Other groupings are much more easily detected, monitored, and controlled, by virtue of the definable types being separated.
>
> There are a number of management devices which are used for control purposes, and I would be loathe to part with any of them, but the foundation is the division by personality groupings.
>
> To begin with, the Situational-Normal group (Group III). These men have individual problems, but by living together and being shielded from the other types, they are spared the necessity of choosing up sides. They don't need to defend the weak or join with the predators. Both [their] dislikes and aggressive acts are ordinarily on an individual basis and can be dealt with that way. While these men may be impulsive, they respond well to counseling and to elementary reinforcement methods. In the two years we have been here, the only cross-unit problems I can recall with this group are a few who have been persuaded or coerced to join [a militant religious group], and one who [became involved in a non-conventional life-style].
>
> The Passive-Inadequate unit (Groups IV & V) has the need for, and has received, sanctuary. By virtue of the homogeneous make-up of the unit, there has been no predatory behavior and any member of it can find safety and security, if he chooses, by remaining in his building. Many, in the early weeks of their stay, choose to remain largely in their own rooms. Later they feel comfortable in the day room and eventually are able to spend some of their free time in more active areas. Were these people indiscriminately mingled with the others here, particularly in view of our multitude of unobservable areas, we could never protect them, nor could we prevent a host of serious

group problems.

The Aggressive-Manipulative group (Groups I & II), because they are all together, is surprisingly easy to handle. On the one hand, they bother each other very little, apparently out of mutual respect. Only once have they presented a group challenge to the administration, and the confrontation that was very narrowly averted as a result apparently lingers in group memory and has a salutary effect. As the saying goes, they can count the house. There is no meaningful support for them in any other unit. The result is that if a group disturbance or confrontation is forced—and this is the unit most likely to do that—they are isolated tactically, geographically, and psychologically.

To this basic framework, which of course is based on your [Quay's] work, we have been able to add embellishments in the form of a transactional analysis unit and a unit based on Carkhuff's (1969, 1973) principles. These are possible, however, only because we have a stable, viable organization to begin with, through the management of typological units.[12]

Another warden, subsequently assigned to the same institution, reported similar positive results: "The typology continues to be an excellent method of placing inmates into homogeneous living units. Thus, this has a tendency to reduce the conflicts in the units. Here is an excellent management tool."[13]

As of this writing the behavioral classification system is used in six institutions of the Federal Bureau of Prisons. In a survey conducted by the Bureau, administrators at these six facilities all reported positive feelings about the approach and indicated that it served to facilitate effective management.[14]

While "hard data" on the utility of the AIMS classification approach to institutional organization are limited, the available material, coupled with the informed opinions of prison administrators, suggests that this behavioral classification method can be useful in reducing inmate violence and facilitating effective management.

NOTES

1. $X^2 = .67$; $df = 1$, $.50 > p > .25$. In actuality, the target facility was somewhat worse in this respect than its sister penitentiaries.

2. $X^2 = 13.66$; $df = 1$, $p < .001$.

3. $X^2 = 5.15$; $.03 > p > .02$.

4. $X^2 = 15.38$; $df = 1$, $p < .001$.

5. $X^2 = 7.39$; $df = 1$, $p < .01$.

6. $X^2 = 4.64$; $df = 1$, $.05 > p > .02$.

7. $X^2 = 16.43$; $df = 1$, $p < .001$.

8. $X^2 = 2.75$; $df = 1$, $p > .05$.

9. $X^2 = 8.70$; $df = 1$, $p < .01$, and $X^2 = 11.97$; $df = 1$, $p < .001$.

10. During those years, the consensus among officials at the Bureau of Prisons was that increased use of diversion and community programming had resulted in a greater proportion of more aggressive inmates being in institutional settings.

11. Bohn (1979, p.58) also reported a reduction of inmate violence with the establishment of a classification system based on the MMPI but presented no data.

12. Charles Fenton, Warden, Federal Correctional Institution, Oxford, Wisconsin, personal communication, June 3, 1975.

13. Larry Kerr, Warden, Federal Correctional Institution, Oxford, Wisconsin, personal communication, July 1982.

14. Robert B. Levinson, Deputy Assistant Director, Bureau of Prisons, personal communication, July 1983.

> "The (Heavy) group, because they are all together, is surprisingly easy to handle... they bother each other very little, and there is no meaningful support for them in any other unit."

5. Comparison With Other Classification Systems

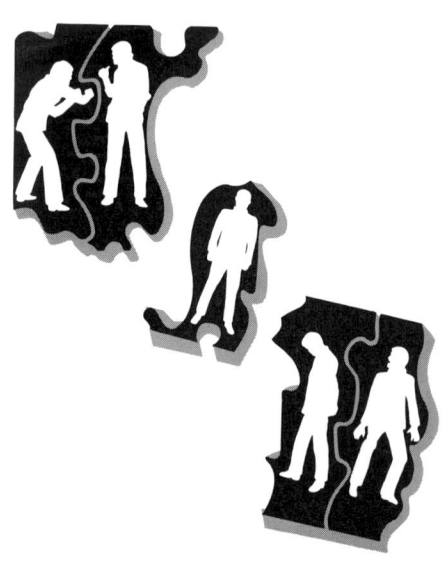

Recent years have seen the development of a number of methods for assessing and classifying offenders for such purposes as meeting security needs, establishing custody levels, parole prediction, management, and treatment. Classification decisions arising from several different systems have been obtained, and results from various samples have been compared with the AIMS behavioral classification approach.

Generally, the data suggest that the "extreme" groups are associated with similar ends-of-the-spectrum groups in the three other systems (security, custody, parole risk) in use in the Federal Bureau of Prisons (Figure 4). However, the overall degree of this association does not reach a level that would make the behavioral classification approach and these other systems interchangeable.

Figure 4
Comparison of Security–Level Implications

Federal*	NIC**	AIMS
6	Maximum	
5 4	Close	Groups I & II
3 2	Medium	Groups IV & V
1	Minimum	Group III

*Bureau of Prisons (1979)
**National Institute of Corrections (1981)

Security Classification

Before designating an incoming offender to a specific correctional institution, the Federal Bureau of Prisons calculates the security level (Stage I in Figure 1)—physical constraint—needed by the individual, ranging from a low of 1 to a high of 6. This determination establishes what type of facility should receive the inmate.

Using a sample of 252 offenders, Table 3 presents a cross-comparison between five BOP security levels (no inmate was classified as level 6) and three housing groups—Heavies (I & II), Moderates (III), and Lights (IV & V). The resulting analysis[1] indicated a statistically significant association between security level and the AIMS approach. Twenty percent of Group III fell in security level 1, as compared to 19% of Group IV & V and 5% of Group I & II. Conversely, only 21% of Group III fell into security levels 4 and 5, as contrasted with 29% of Group IV & V and 38% of Group I & II. Thus, as would be expected, the Moderate group tends to be highly represented among the minimum security offenders—53% (20/38)—and have limited presence within the maximum security prisoner category. The reverse is true, as would be anticipated, for the Heavy group, which represented 42% (30/72) of the inmates needing maximum security.

Custody Classification

The Federal Bureau of Prisons has also implemented a system for classifying in-

Table 3
Cross-comparison of AIMS Groups and Bureau of Prisons Security Levels

	Group			
	I & II	III	IV & V	Total
Security level	N (%)	N (%)	N (%)	N (%)
1 (minimum)	4 (5)	20 (20)	14 (19)	38 (15)
2 (medium)	22 (28)	30 (30)	13 (18)	65 (26)
3 (medium)	23 (29)	29 (29)	25 (34)	77 (31)
4 (maximum)	25 (32)	20 (20)	19 (26)	64 (25)
5 (maximum)	5 (6)	1 (1)	2 (3)	8 (3)
	79 (31)	100 (40)	73 (29)	252 (100)

> The Moderate group tends to be highly represented among the minimum security offenders.... The reverse is true, as would be anticipated, for the Heavy group.

coming offenders with regard to level of custody; that is, the degree of supervision deemed appropriate for each individual (Stage III in Figure 1). The four custody levels are: *close, in, out,* and *community*.[2]

Table 4 cross-classifies custody level and AIMS group membership for 258 offenders at a single institution that also housed its inmates in three groups—I & II, III, and IV & V. This contingency table again indicates a statistically significant degree of association between the two classification methods.[3]

Ninety percent of the Heavies (combined Groups I & II) were *in* custody (this facility's highest level of supervision) compared to 71% of the Lights (Groups IV & V) and 56% of the Moderates (Group III). *Community* custody included 0% of the I & II group, 4% of the IV & V group, but 15% of Group III.

As was the case for security needs, the custody data strongly support the expected outcomes: the Heavy group is

Table 4
Cross-comparison of AIMS Groups and Bureau of Prisons Custody Levels

	Group			
	I & II	III	IV & V	Total
Custody level*	N (%)	N (%)	N (%)	N (%)
In	71 (90)	60 (56)	51 (71)	182 (71)
Out	8 (10)	31 (29)	18 (25)	57 (22)
Community	0 (0)	16 (15)	3 (4)	19 (7)
	79 (31)	107 (41)	72 (28)	258 (100)

* This facility does not have *close* custody inmates.

Table 5
Cross-comparison of AIMS Groups and U.S. Parole Commission Salient Factor Scores

Salient factor category (score)	Group I N (%)	II N (%)	III N (%)	IV N (%)	V N (%)	Total N (%)
Very good risk (High 8+)	10 (10)	16 (44)	54 (64)	27 (40)	11 (37)	118 (37)
Good risk (Medium-high 6–7)	27 (26)	6 (17)	2 (25)	14 (20)	7 (23)	75 (23)
Fair risk (Medium-low 4–5)	35 (33)	8 (22)	4 (5)	16 (24)	8 (27)	71 (22)
Poor risk (Low 0–3)	33 (31)	6 (17)	5 (6)	11 (16)	4 (13)	59 (18)
	105 (33)	36 (11)	84 (26)	68 (21)	30 (9)	323 (100)

underrepresented in the *community* custody level—0% (0/19)—and has the greatest presence in the most restrictive supervision level—49% (70/182).

Salient Factor Scores

The U.S. Parole Commission uses a parole risk prediction formula as part of its process for determining time to be served prior to eligibility for parole. This "salient factor" score is made up of items involving prior convictions, prior incarcerations, age at first arrest, type of offense, history of parole revocation, drug use, education, employment history, and release plan. (The items related to previous incarcerations and employment overlap with two similar items on the Life History Checklist that are scored for Scale I). The salient factor score can be thought of as a classification that, by Parole Commission standards, separates offenders into four parole risk classes: *very good, good, fair,* and *poor.*

Table 5 presents a cross-comparison between these four classes of salient factor scores and the five behavioral classification groups. The highly statistically significant association[4] was due primarily to the accumulation of Group I cases (64%) in the two lower (unfavorable) salient factor score categories and the concentration of Group III cases (89%) in the two more favorable risk categories. The other three AIMS groups were not systematically distributed.

Although it composed only 26% of the sample, Group III represented 43% (54/118) of the cases in the *very good* risk category; whereas Group I, while representing 33% of the total sample, made up 56% (33/59) of the *poor* risk category.

Because salient factor scores can be considered to be continuous measures, an analysis of variance was performed comparing the mean scores for the five groups. The mean for Group I was significantly lower (Duncan procedure, $p = .05$) — poorer risk — than those of the other groups, while the Group III mean was significantly higher. Groups II, IV, and V did not differ among themselves.

As a consequence of the significant difference between the salient factor scores of Groups I and III, the data were further analyzed by a discriminant function. The use of the salient factor score to predict group membership was quite successful in the case of both Groups I and III—membership was correctly predicted for 79% of both groups. However, membership for Groups II, IV, and V was not predicted well, as these cases were all assigned (about equally) to Groups I or III. Group identification for all five AIMS groups was correctly predicted by salient factor score in only 46% of the cases (149/323).

Summary

The comparisons between the Adult Internal Management System and three other methods for assessing offenders were all supportive—in every instance the results were in the expected direction. These findings lend credence to the usefulness of AIMS as an effective management device.

Notes

1. $X^2 = 15.77$; df = 8, p = .05.

2. *Close* custody means the inmate requires virtually continuous supervision. This custody is for individuals who by their behavior have identified themselves as assaultive, predatory, riotous, or serious escape risks, thereby demonstrating their inability to associate with the general prisoner population without becoming dangerous to the well-being of others or disruptive to the orderly running of the facility. When not in their secure cells, these individuals are restricted to designated (more secure) areas within the prison and kept under close staff surveillance. Within these constraints they can participate in available institutional programs and work assignments.

In custody means the prisoner is assigned to regular housing quarters; e.g., a single cell/room but may be double bunked (a multiple cell or squad rooms might also be appropriate). These inmates are eligible for all program activities inside the institution's secure perimeter and under normal levels of supervision, but *not* for work or program assignments outside.

Out custody means the inmate may be assigned to less secure housing quarters within the institution; i.e., open dorms, cubicles, or rooms. With intermittent supervision, these individuals are eligible for work details and program assignments outside the facility's secure perimeter.

Community custody means the offender is eligible for the least secure of living quarters, including housing outside the facility's perimeter. These inmates may work on outside work details or program assignments with minimal supervision and are eligible to participate in community-based program activities.

3. $X^2 = 27.06$; df = 4, p <.001.

4. $X^2 = 76.15$; df = 12, p = .0001.

—in every instance, the results were in the expected direction.

6. Implications for Correctional Practice

> The system is reasonably easy to implement and, in contrast to some other approaches, does not depend on the cooperation of each inmate.

At this writing, some 15 years after its development, the AIMS behavioral classification system has been shown to be a valid and useful approach for grouping adult male offenders for management purposes (see Part II, Technical Data). This system is reasonably easy to implement and, in contrast to some other approaches, does not depend on the cooperation of each inmate.

In-Institution Practice

The validity and utility of the behavioral classification system has implications for the total classification process. For example, the validity of the Life History Checklist is a function of the accuracy and completeness of the offender's social history. Such histories are rarely if ever taken with completion of the CALH in mind; rather, they tend to reflect the preconceptions of both correctional agencies and individual probation officers, caseworkers, and others about what is important. Systematizing history-taking to include all the information needed to complete the Life History Checklist can only increase the precision of the classification process.

Similarly, admissions and orientation units are rarely organized to permit observation and assessment of the newly admitted inmate by concerned, trained staff. Making certain that sufficient time and opportunity are provided for valid observation can increase the validity not only of the Adjustment Checklist ratings, but, again, of the total classification process as well.

System-Wide Practice

Thought might profitably be given to the question of why every institution in a given department of corrections should try to deal with all five behavioral groups, as is now almost universally the case. For example, Group III inmates offer relatively few management problems (and might present even fewer in the most appropriate environment). Moreover, their post-release behavior is rarely seriously criminal. Prisoners in this group might well benefit most from an open, education- and industry-oriented setting dedicated solely to their needs. Such an environment would likely require a minimum of custody-oriented staff, would not need to be built with control in mind, and therefore should be more economical per capita both to construct and to operate than institutions that try to serve all groups.

Offenders in Groups IV & V appear to have specialized needs. While little data exist, the impression gained by a number of administrators and researchers is that both of these groups are disproportionately involved with drugs and alcohol. Specialized facilities that offer the necessary degree of control while concentrating on methods for ameliorating drug and alcohol misuse (and other psychological problems) might be the most appropriate means of intervention—particularly for any inmates in those two groups known to be involved in substance abuse.

Group I & II inmates pose serious problems for all facets of the criminal justice system. They are not only the earliest to become involved in criminality, they are the most persistent offenders and the ones most likely to commit violent offenses. These prisoners also present severe management problems in correctional settings. At the same time, many of them (60% in our sample, see Section 8) did *not* recidivate and were not serious management problems while in prison. It is possible that a sharpening of the Adjustment and Life History checklists, along with the possible addition of other assessment techniques, might permit the most troublesome members within Groups I & II to be separated into a distinct subgroup. Further correctional research into this most problematic area is clearly warranted.

Conclusion

As suggested at the outset of this part of the manual, the Adult Internal Management System is one aspect of a total approach to inmate classification. Each individual entering a correctional system proceeds through a number of sorting procedures:

• determining the level of security the new arrival needs in order to adequately protect society; i.e., security designation;

• establishing the level of supervision the offender requires in order to maintain an appropriate level of control; i.e., custody level assignment;

• assigning the inmate's housing area in a manner that will reduce internal management problems and inter-prisoner conflicts; i.e., internal management classification; and

• developing an individualized schedule of program activities that will keep an inmate productively occupied during incarceration and better prepare the offender to succeed following return to the community.

Each of these functions is carried out at some level of explicitness in all correctional systems. To the degree that they are accomplished in a consistent, rational, objective manner, corrections will function in a more effective and cost-efficient fashion.

It should be recognized that just to "group" inmates is not enough. While not minimizing the significance of this function, it is only the first important step in a comprehensive correctional process. Grouping prisoners by behaviorally relevant variables will reduce problems for both staff and inmates. Having accomplished that, the next step is differential programming. As many experienced correctional personnel are aware, there are no panaceas. No single program works at a highly effective level with all prisoners. Homogeneously grouping offenders assists in identifying which program is appropriate for whom. Once the most appropriate target group has been discovered, the third step is assuring the delivery of a quality program.

Some institutions that have implemented AIMS also created treatment programs to meet the needs of certain groups. In addition, inmates from all groups were permitted to self-select themselves into other specialized treatment programs. Complete data on these special activities have not yet been fully analyzed. When the effects of those programs, if any, are related to post-release behavior, there may be more to say about the usefulness of AIMS as a basis for both differential treatment and management.

Regardless of which correctional philosophy one adheres to—deterrence, incapacitation, punishment, or rehabilitation—it is evident that the vast majority of today's prisoners will return to our community on some tomorrow. What kind of an individual will be walking the streets is contingent in large measure upon that person's experience while incarcerated. Inhumane treatment "inside" breeds bitterness and a will to get even once "outside." To the degree that prisons are safe and humane institutions, all of us benefit.

> **Just to "group" inmates is not enough...it is only the first important step in a comprehensive correctional process.**

Part II. Technical Data

Section 7. Development of the System

Section 8. Reliability and Validity

7. Development of the System

The development of the Adult Internal Management System was a natural extension of earlier work that resulted in a behavioral classification approach for juveniles (Quay & Parsons, 1971). That system was first used at the Federal Youth Center, Morgantown, West Virginia (Gerard, 1970). The methods used to develop the adult version were basically the same as those used for the juveniles but with some improvements.

The purpose of the initial research effort with AIMS was to discover, through use of factor analytic techniques, the broadband dimensions of behavior and attitudes characterizing adult prisoners (approximately ages 18 to 45). Simultaneously, instruments were sought for measuring these dimensions and techniques were devised for classifying adult male inmates into behaviorally homogeneous groups.

Initially, as had been the case in the development of the juvenile system, the behavioral data collected were based on (1) observation of behavior in the correctional setting, (2) the offender's life (social) history, and (3) the inmate's responses to a specially constructed self-report personality inventory. Early efforts with the inventory were not productive, however. In addition, use of personality questionnaires had come under critical scrutiny. Consequently, research on the personality inventory was not vigorously pursued and is not reported herein.

Rating Current Inmate Behavior: The Correctional Adjustment Checklist (CACL)

Construction of the Item Pool

To cover as adequately as possible the domain of behaviors that might forecast adjustment and program participation in correctional settings, a large pool of descriptors was sought. Items describing relevant behavior were solicited from the staff of a number of institutions as well as from mental health professionals with correctional experience. Items were also adapted from previous research with juveniles.

The elimination of synonyms and descriptors of behaviors that would have very low frequencies of occurrence in correctional institutions resulted in a preliminary checklist containing 81 items.

Ratings

Ratings of inmate behavior were obtained from line staff whose positions gave them good knowledge of the characteristics of those prisoners selected to be observed. In most cases the raters were correctional officers or correctional counselors[1] in admissions units. Due to the scope of the project, no training could be undertaken beyond familiarizing these staff with the instrument and answering initial questions.

Subjects

Three separate subject pools were used (Appendix 9). The first two samples—A&B—were obtained from the indicated federal correctional institutions by taking all new admissions, transfers, and parole violators who had previously been in some other institution. The third sample—C—was obtained from a survey of four facilities used to identify a group of prisoners whose characteristics (age under 30 with sentences of six years or longer) made them eligible for transfer to the then-newly-opened Federal Correctional Institution in Oxford, Wisconsin.

These inmate samples provided a representative cross-section of adult male federal prisoners, ranging from those appropriate for an open, minimum security facility (Seagoville) through medium security correctional institutions (El Reno, Milan, Petersburg, Tallahassee) to maximum security penitentiaries (Atlanta, Lewisburg, Lompoc, McNeil, Terre Haute, and Marion, which is the Federal Prison System's most maximally secure facility).

Since the data analysis was to focus on the extraction of homogeneous subsets of characteristics based on statistical association (correlation), the first evaluation used only those subjects about whom at least four of the items on the Correctional Adjustment Checklist had been rated as being present. This resulted in the loss of about 200 subjects who did not meet this criterion.

> The intent of the checklists is to cover as adequately as possible the domain of behaviors that might forecast adjustment and program participation in correctional settings.

Factor Analytic Procedures

Factor analysis was accomplished using (1) R^2 as the initial communality estimate, (2) a drop in the eigenvalue to less than 1 as the criterion of when to stop factoring, and (3) the varimax rotation. No variable was entered into the correlation matrix if its frequency was less than 10% or more than 90%; in the majority of cases the split was much less than these extreme values.

not appearing on the initial version of the Adjustment Checklist are noted with an asterisk in Appendix 10.

Three principal dimensions emerged in all three analyses. The first (Scale I) reflected toughness, defiance, physical and verbal aggression, trouble-making, victimizing, and having a quick temper.

The second dimension (Scale IV)[2] was composed of such behaviors as inability to follow directions, sluggishness,

Table 6
Congruency Coefficients for Correctional Adjustment Checklist (CACL)

Sample B factors	Sample A factors			
	I	II	IV	V
I	**.85**		.15	.16
IV	.46		**.53**	.33
V	.02		−.03	**.73**

Sample C factors	Sample A factors			
	I	II	IV	V
I	**.96**	.75	.33	.06
II	.66	**.84**	.19	.21
IV	.35	−.46	**.76**	.36
V	.23	−.33	.17	**.23**

Sample B factors	Sample C factors			
	I	II	IV	V
I	**.84**		.39	.24
IV	.22		**.67**	.35
V	.24		.61	**.58**

Factorial Dimensions

Rotated factor loadings from all three analyses are presented in Appendix 10. Items that did not meet the frequency criterion or did not load on any of the factors were dropped subsequent to the first analysis. Other descriptors were added for a second analysis; those items daydreaming, preoccupation, passivity, moodiness, and dullness.

The third factor (Scale V)[3] reflected worry, tenseness, help-seeking, fear of other inmates, sadness, and emotional lability.

The fourth factor appeared in only two of the samples; it was measured by only five items (Scale II) and encompassed such characteristics as trying to con staff, lack of trust in staff, accusing staff of unfairness, and playing staff off against one another.

FACTORIAL INVARIANCE

The degree to which the scales (factors) from the three separate analyses were related to one another was assessed by computing Tucker's congruency coefficients (see Harman, 1970, pp. 269-270); the findings are presented in Table 6. In all cases the match for Scale I is excellent. Although Scales I and II clearly were similar, in the two samples (A and C) from which Scale II emerged, the congruence was excellent. Congruence for the Scale IV factor was also very good. The matches for Scale V were weaker, especially with respect to samples A vs. C. The congruence of Scale V was good for samples A vs. B and samples B vs. C.

ADJUSTMENT CHECKLIST SCALES

Item selection. Descriptors were selected for inclusion in the final scales based on two criteria: (1) the magnitude of the loading of the item on its respective factor in one or more of the three analyses, and (2) the relative consistency of the item as a measure of the factor across the three analyses. Although there were some exceptions, as a general rule a descriptor was selected only if it appeared on its respective scale in two of the three analyses *and* only if its average loading was at least .40. Appendix 11 shows the items on the final form of the CACL[4] and indicates the scale to which each item belongs.

Psychometric characteristics. To assess each scale's various psychometric properties, scale (factor) scores were computed using unit weights for all 829 subjects in the combined samples. For each item checked as characteristic of an inmate, a value of one point was earned toward the score on that factor; thus the maximum possible score for each scale was the number of items it contained.

The raw score distributions revealed rather gross departures from normality for all four scales (Appendixes 12-15). Consequently, the next step required was to produce normalized T-scores for each possible raw score. Conversion tables for transforming each raw score into a normalized T-score are found in Appendix 16.

Scale intercorrelations. While the factor analytic procedure used results in uncorrelated factors, the actual estimates of scores obtained by individuals on those factors are not necessarily independent. The intercorrelations among the scale scores are presented in Table 7. Scales I and II are substantially correlated; this is undoubtedly due to the fact that they both represent facets, albeit factorially distinct, of acting-out behavior. Thus

Table 7
Intercorrelations Among Correctional Adjustment Checklist (CACL) Scale Scores

	Scales		
Scales	II	IV	V
I	.68	.33	.12
II		.28	.10
IV			.48

high scorers on Scale I will tend to obtain elevated scores on Scale II. Similarly, Scales IV and V are modestly related, since both factors reflect a dimension of nonaggressiveness towards others.

ANALYZING OFFENDER RECORDS: CHECKLIST FOR THE ANALYSIS OF LIFE HISTORY RECORDS OF ADULT OFFENDERS (CALH)

CONSTRUCTION OF THE ITEM POOL

In selecting items for inclusion in the initial analysis, the intent was to sample behavior and personal characteristics

that would (or should) be mentioned in presentence reports (or elicited during casework interviews) and that would, at least in theory, have a bearing on degree of institutional adjustment and program participation. Main sources for descriptors were a sample of presentence reports and the results of previous work with juveniles. The initial form of the Life History Checklist contained 67 items.

RATINGS

In the vast majority of cases, ratings were made by institutional case managers based on presentence reports, other collateral data that might have been available in records, and any additional knowledge about the inmate's history elicited during interviews.

SUBJECTS

Two separate subject pools were used (Appendix 17). The two samples were obtained from the cooperating institutions by using all new admissions, transfers, and parole violators who had previously been in some other institution.

As in the case of the Correctional Adjustment Checklist, representation from different types of federal institutions was obtained. Again, since statistical association among the life history items was being sought, only those subjects were used about whom at least four of the items had been rated as present. This criterion resulted in the loss of fewer than 50 out of the total pool of 2,231 available subjects.

FACTOR ANALYTIC PROCEDURES

Procedures were identical to those described for the Correctional Adjustment Checklist. The samples are as shown in Appendix 17.

FACTORIAL DIMENSIONS

Rotated factor loadings from the two analyses are presented in Appendix 18. As was the case with the Adjustment Checklist, life history items that failed to meet the 10%-90% frequency criterion or to load on a factor in the first analysis were dropped for the second evaluation.

Because the original item pool was considered exhaustive, no attempt was made to add descriptors during a second analysis.

Three principal scales (factors) emerged in both analyses. Factor I (now Scale I) reflected a history of physical aggression, thrill-seeking, uncontrollability, toughness, defiance, unresponsiveness to counseling, and other aspects of an overt aggressive behavior pattern.

Factor II (now Scale IV) included such characteristics as lack of friends, preoccupation, social withdrawal, indecisiveness, incompetence, and passivity.

Factor III (now Scale III) contained only six items common to both analyses: has expressed guilt over offense; has expressed need for self-improvement; has supported wife and children; claims offense was motivated by family problems; has a single marriage; and has suffered financial reverses prior to offense. These characteristics suggest a basically normal individual who most likely offended out of some immediate precipitating environmental stress.

FACTORIAL INVARIANCE

To assess the comparability of the factors obtained from the two analyses, congruency coefficients were again computed (Table 8). The relationships between like-named scales were all .80 or

Table 8 Congruency Coefficients for Life History Checklist (CALH)			
	Sample A scales		
Sample B scales	I	III	IV
I	.88	−.28	.38
III	.05	.80	−.32
IV	−.55	−.31	.88

above, while relationships among the unlike scales were much lower. A satisfactory match clearly existed for all three factors.

LIFE HISTORY CHECKLIST SCALES

Item selection. As was the case with

the Adjustment Checklist items, the final scales of the Life History Checklist were selected on the basis of the size of their factor loadings and the consistency of an item's appearance in both analyses. Twelve items with an average loading of .41 were selected for Scale I; only six items with an average loading of .37 were adequate for inclusion in Scale III; nine items with an average loading of .38 were chosen for Scale IV. The descriptors on the final form of the CALH are shown in Appendix 19.[5]

Psychometric characteristics. Life History scale scores based on unit weights (one point for each item checked on the three scales) were obtained for all subjects in the second sample. Raw score distributions were plotted and, as in the case of the Adjustment Checklist, rather gross departures from normality were observed (Appendix 20). Therefore, normalized T-scores were again generated; the raw scores and their T-score equivalents are given in Appendix 21.

Scale intercorrelations. As noted previously, while the factor analytic method produces uncorrelated dimensions, the actual scores obtained by a set of individuals are estimates of their true factor score and thus may be correlated. The obtained intercorrelations of the scores on the three scales of the Life History Checklist were: I vs. IV, r = .14; I vs. III, r = -.33; and III vs. IV, r = .10. With the exception of the negative relationship between Scales I and III, no meaningful relationships existed among the three CALH scales.

INTERRELATIONSHIPS AMONG CHECKLIST SCALES

In the process of gathering data from the second sample (for the development of both the CACL and CALH), ratings on the two instruments were obtained on a subset of 502 subjects. This permitted correlations to be calculated between the scales of both instruments (Table 9). The values of greatest interest were those obtained between like-named scales. These values (.32 for Scale I and .15 for Scale IV), while disappointingly low, were not unlike values obtained in similar comparisons among same-named scales for the measurement of behavioral dimensions in juveniles (see Quay & Parsons, 1971).

**Table 9
Intercorrelations Among CACL and CALH Scales**

CACL	CALH I	CALH III	CALH IV
I	.32	-.22	.04
II	.27	-.19	.00
IV	.09	.00	.15
V	.02	.08	.08

NOTES

1. A correctional counselor is an experienced correctional officer who has received specialized training in counseling techniques and is assigned a group of inmates to work with during an extended period of time. Counselors may work with offenders on a one-to-one basis or in group sessions; their focus is on the inmates' day-to-day problems associated with living in a correctional institution.

2. In the earliest version of this manual, what is now Scale IV was initially labeled Scale III.

3. What is now Scale V was initially labeled Scale IV in the earliest version of this manual.

4. Some earlier versions of the CACL possibly still in use contain 63 items, 22 of which are not scored on any scale.

5. Some earlier versions of the CALH possibly in current use contain 50 items, 23 of which are not scored on any scale.

8. Reliability and Validity

> —a measure cannot relate to something else (validity) to a greater extent than it relates to itself (reliability).

Reliability

Reliability is important primarily for its effect on validity: a classification system cannot be valid without being reliable. Put another way, reliability has to do with the relationship of a measure to itself—a measure cannot relate to something else (validity) to a greater extent than it relates to itself.

Psychometric theory recognizes three general types of reliability: internal consistency, inter-rater, and rate-rerate (stability). For purposes of assessing the reliability of the AIMS approach, internal consistency reliability was of major importance in order to demonstrate that the scales of both the Adjustment and Life History checklists were satisfactorily homogeneous. The internal consistency of both instruments was assessed using Cronbach's alpha. In a sample of 829 cases, the obtained values for the CACL were .91 for Scale I, .77 for Scale II, .82 for Scale IV, and .77 for Scale V. For the CALH the obtained reliabilities were .72 for Scale I, .57 for Scale III, and .57 for Scale IV.

Neither inter-rater nor stability reliability has been obtained for the scales. However, the validity of the system, as demonstrated in the following pages, argues for those types of reliabilities as well.

Validity

Validity—the degree to which an instrument actually assesses that which it is designed to measure—is not the simple concept it might seem. The field of psychological measurement recognizes a number of different kinds of validity. The most direct type is known as concur-

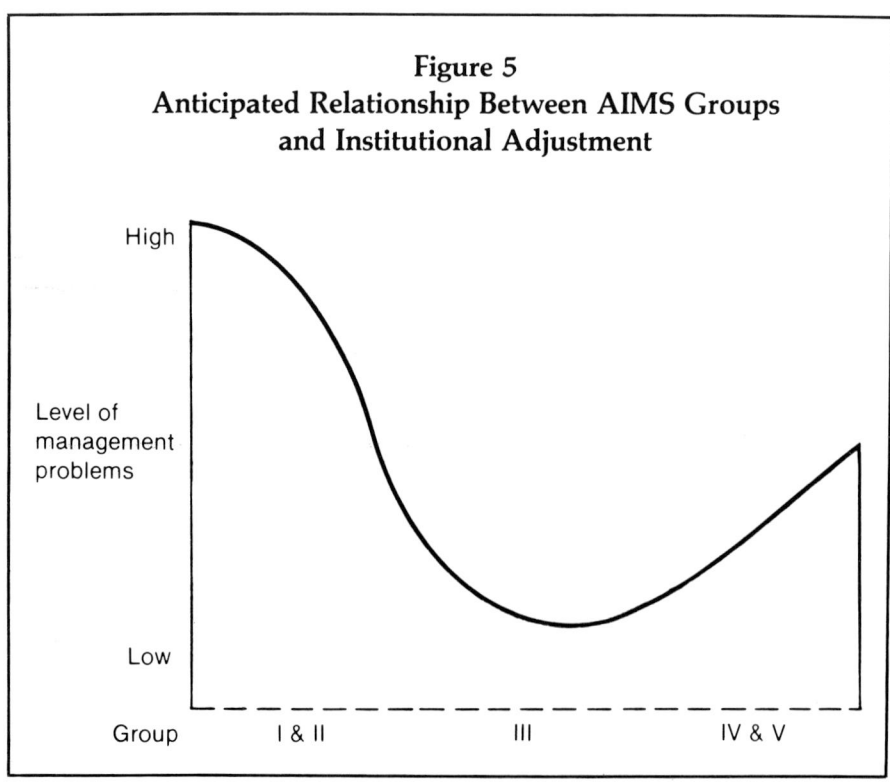

Figure 5
Anticipated Relationship Between AIMS Groups and Institutional Adjustment

Table 10
Significant Correlations Between CACL and CALH Scales and Other Variables

Variable and its (mean)	CACL				CALH		
	I	II	IV	V	I	III	IV
Age (26.1)	−.22		−.22		.31		−.18
Race					.32		
SAT median (8.4)			−.19				
IQ (105.5)			−.29				−.20
Income per month ($493)					−.29	.22	
Area of residence		−.20					
Previous arrests (5.9)		−.19			.47		
Previous incarcerations (.76)					.64	−.27	.20
Age at first arrest (19.5)			−.33		−.42	.29	−.19

rent validity; this refers to the degree to which one assessment device for a psychological characteristic correlates with another measure—the criterion—whose validity is *prima facie* or already established. For example, a newly developed intelligence test is expected to correlate with an older, already established instrument. In the case of AIMS, however, there is no older established measure of the five offender groups. Thus there are no concurrent criteria against which to correlate the results obtained from the Adjustment and Life History checklists.

Other types of validity, however, are relevant for this system. One of these, construct validity, is a more complex notion than concurrent validity. Basically, construct validity refers to the extent to which a measure relates to other measures in predictable and logical ways. In the case of AIMS, if we classify a group of inmates as belonging in Group I, we are saying that those prisoners manifest aggressive and hostile behavior, that they are rule-breakers and more likely to be violent, etc. If such is indeed the case, then those classified as being in Group I should differ in a variety of predictable ways from, say, those in Group III, whom we describe very differently. Group I inmates, for example, should be found in greater proportion in maximum security than in open institutions; they should also accumulate more disciplinary infractions and show poorer in-institution work performance (see Figure 5).

The process of establishing the construct validity of AIMS involves examining a host of correlates of group membership. Whenever a relationship is in the predicted direction, evidence for construct validity is added; doubt is cast when an observed relationship runs counter to the prediction (e.g., if those in Group I had fewer rule infractions than those in Group III). What must be recognized is that no *single* relationship allows one to say that the system, or some part of it, is either valid or invalid. Judgment must be made on the basis of a series of confirmations or disconfirmations.

Another important point to acknowledge is that the strength of relationships between aspects of this classification system and other relevant variables not only is a function of the validity of AIMS but is dependent as well on the reliability with which the other variable is measured. If an institution monitors and records rule infractions haphazardly, then these become unreliable criteria against which to judge the validity of anything. Unfortunately, much of the data (supposedly) routinely collected in correctional settings are often of unknown reliability; in some instances they are strongly suspect of being unreliable.

Construct Validity of AIMS

Over the years during which the Adult Internal Management System was being developed and put into use, a considerable amount of data was collected bearing on its construct validity. The earliest analysis related the scale scores on the Adjustment and Life History checklists to information obtained concerning 100 consecutive admissions to the Federal Correctional Institution, Seagoville, Texas. Significant correlations ($p < .05$) between the scales and other variables are given in Table 10.

It was anticipated that the various scales would be differentially related to these other variables in logical and meaningful ways. By and large this was the case. Those with high Scale I scores tended to be younger, have a smaller monthly income, to have had more previous arrests and incarcerations, and to have been younger at time of first arrest. With regard to the correlation (.64) with number of previous incarcerations, it should be noted that one of the twelve items on Scale I of the Life History

Checklist refers to the presence of one or more previous incarcerations in the inmate's background; therefore this obtained relationship was not completely independent.

Scale II scores were related to urban residence and fewer prior arrests. This suggested a tendency for Group II offenders to be city dwellers and, possibly, to have been fairly successful at avoiding contact with law enforcement agencies.

Scores on Scale III were related to being older, being white, and having had a higher monthly income, fewer prior incarcerations, and a first arrest at an older age.

Higher scores on Scale IV were associated with being younger, less academically accomplished, less intelligent, having more prior incarcerations, and being younger at time of first arrest.

Although the statistically significant relationships obtained were modest in magnitude, all were in the expected direction and reflect positively on the construct validity of the scales. Equally important, the obtained correlations were too low to permit prediction of scale scores (and thus group membership) solely on the basis of age, race, IQ, or area of residence.

Additional data relevant to the construct validity of AIMS were collected over a period of three years on large samples of offenders in two federal prisons. One institution was a newly opened medium (MED) security facility for younger, long-sentence offenders primarily from the upper Midwest. The other was a minimum (MIN) security open facility in the Southwest. Inmates were classified upon entry into these

> What must be recognized is that no *single* relationship allows one to say that the system, or some part of it, is either valid or invalid. Judgment must be made on the basis of a series of confirmations or disconfirmations.

Table 11
Ethnic Distribution by AIMS Group
(Two Institutions)
(N = 1,394)

Ethnic background	Group				
	I	II	III	IV	V
Caucasian	22.1%	13.0%	34.8%	22.8%	7.5%
Black	39.9	16.0	23.1	17.5	3.5
Latin	13.0	10.3	44.8	29.1	2.7

Table 12
Age Distribution by AIMS Group
(Two Institutions)
(N = 1,598)

Age range	Group					Total sample
	I	II	III	IV	V	
17 - 23	34.6%	29.3%	21.3%	29.8%	33.7%	30.0%
23 - 28	44.3	48.6	46.3	48.0	49.4	45.2
28 - 33	15.8	15.8	20.7	17.3	11.2	17.2
33 - 38	4.4	4.5	8.0	4.9	2.2	5.5
38 - 43	0.7	1.4	2.8	0.0	1.1	1.4
43 and over	0.2	0.5	0.9	0.0	2.2	0.7

prisons. Various psychological tests were also administered, and in-program performance was monitored.

Appendix 22 shows the distribution of cases classified into the five groups by the methods described in Part I of this manual. The data indicate, as would be expected, that MIN had proportionately fewer cases than MED in Group I (22% v. 34%) and proportionately more cases in Groups III (35% vs. 27%) and IV (27% vs. 18%) ($X^2 = 155.1$; df = 4, p < .001). Thus, these data lend credibility to the construct validity of AIMS.

ship of age to group membership are contained in Table 12. These data confirm the earlier finding of a modest relationship between classification and age, with younger inmates tending to fall in Group I and somewhat older inmates falling in Group III ($X^2 = 43.69$; df = 20, p < .001).

Table 13
AIMS Group Means and SDs of IQ (Beta) Scores
(N = 1,433)

	Group				
	I	II	III	IV	V
Mean Beta IQ	103.19	106.72	107.81	105.29	106.29
SD	12.59	12.05	11.06	11.92	14.44
N	371	187	371	85	85

Table 14
AIMS Group Means and SDs on MMPI Pd Scale
(N = 1,824)

	Group				
	I	II	III	IV	V
Mean	72.17	69.61	66.06	69.21	67.27
SD	11.35	8.66	10.09	10.94	10.48

> It is clear... that Group I not only incurs the greatest number of disciplinary reports overall—it also receives the most severe ones as well as the highest number involving aggressiveness and noncompliance with institutional regulations.

INMATE DEMOGRAPHICS

Ethnicity. A cross-tabulation of three major ethnic backgrounds and group classification in the two institutions (MIN and MED) is presented in Table 11. The ethnic distribution within the five groups was not random ($X^2 = 82.67$; df = 8, p < .001). There were proportionately more black inmates in Group I and proportionately fewer in Group III; Latins and Caucasians were highly represented in Group III.

Age. Additional data on the relation-

INMATE TEST RESULTS

Intelligence. Table 13 displays the means and SDs (standard deviations) for the five groups on the Revised Beta (nonverbal) intelligence test. While there were statistically significant differences among the means (F = 8.13; df = 4, 1428, p < .001), even the differences between the two most contrasting groups (I vs. III) were of no practical importance since less than five IQ points were involved—well within the test's error of measurement.

The Pd Scale of the MMPI. The Minnesota Multiphasic Personality Inventory (MMPI), a widely used self-report test of deviant personality characteristics, is routinely administered to all incoming inmates in the Federal Prison

System. The Psychopathic Deviate (Pd) subscale measures characteristics of hostility, aggression, and lack of concern for others. Table 14 presents the means and SDs (in T-scores) of the five groups on the Pd scale. The higher the T-score, the more psychopathic characteristics are present; T-scores above 70 are generally interpreted as being significantly in the clinically meaningful range.

The overall difference among the groups was highly significant (F = 17.04; df = 5, 1818, p < .001). As would be expected, Group I significantly exceeded all others, and both Groups II and IV exceeded Group III (p < .05). The clinically significant mean Pd score for Group I supports the validity of AIMS.

IN-PROGRAM BEHAVIOR

In-institution work performance. As part of the Bureau of Prison's research into unit management and classification, inmates were rated regarding their performance on institution job assignments. On the measure utilized (Megargee, 1972; Fowler & Megargee, 1976), higher scores indicate better performance (see Table 15). An analysis of variance indicated an overall difference among the groups (F = 13.03; df = 4, 799, p < .001). Again, adding to the construct validity of AIMS, the contrast between the higher Group III mean score and all other group means was significant (p < .001). The differences in mean scores, however, were very modest in size.

In order to conduct further data analyses bearing on construct validity, a random sample was drawn from the two institutions. Eliminating cases where no AIMS classification had been made (or was indeterminate) resulted in a basic sample of 425 cases—308 from the medium security (MED) prison and 117 from the minimum security (MIN) facility. A comparison among the percentages for the five groups between this random sample and the larger population is presented in Appendix 23. Neither institution showed any statistically significant difference in the relative frequencies of membership in the five AIMS groups. (In the analyses that follow, sample sizes may differ due to the unavailability of data on varying numbers of cases.)

Disciplinary infractions. Individual records were searched for disciplinary infractions routinely recorded according to Bureau of Prisons policy. These misconduct reports were separable into two levels: those handled at the living-unit level (generally less serious) and those of greater severity, which had been adjudicated by an institution-wide disciplinary committee.

A cross-tabulation of both types of infractions by classification group is presented in Tables 16 and 17. To perform X^2 analyses, the number of infractions was clustered in order to provide a statistically acceptable number of cases in each cell in the contingency table.

For MIN, this approach was not entirely successful. More than 20% of the cells continued to have expected frequencies of less than 5, due in part to the small number of subjects in Group V. Dropping Group V did not correct the problem. Moreover, X^2 did not even approach significance for either level of infractions. Thus no relationship was found between group classification and receiving either minor or major disciplinary infractions for institution MIN. It appears, then, that the "best" inmates in all five groups (as would be the case for those living in MIN) are equally successful in avoiding misconduct reports. This also supports the notion that not *all* inmates classified as Group I are troublemakers.

For MED, an analysis of the less severe infractions produced a X^2 of 28.42 (df = 8, p = .004). As predicted, it can be seen in Table 16 that 68% of Group III and 66% of Group V had either none or only one infraction, as compared to 44% of Group I; Groups II and IV occupied an intermediate position. On the other hand, 25% of Group I had five or more infractions, compared to only 6% of Group III and 7% of the much smaller Group V; Groups II and IV again occupied the intermediate position. Overall, Group I had 34% of the disciplinary in-

Table 15
AIMS Group Means and SDs on Megargee In-institution Work Performance Scale
(N = 804)

	Group				
	I	II	III	IV	V
Mean	28.31	27.91	30.83	27.68	27.71
SD	5.61	7.09	4.82	5.29	6.02

fractions; Group V had only 9%. One would have expected each of the five AIMS groups to have had 20% of the total number.

Group differences at MED involving the more severe disciplinary infractions (Table 17) were even more pronounced (X^2 = 29.98; df = 8, p. = .0003). Seventy percent of Group III had no severe misconduct reports, as compared

Table 16
Unit-level (Minor) Disciplinary Infractions by AIMS Group (Two Institutions)

	Group	0 - 1	2 - 4	5 or more	Total by group
MIN	I	18 (64%)	10 (36%)	0 (0%)	28 (24%)
	II	14 (78%)	3 (17%)	1 (6%)	18 (16%)
	III	22 (79%)	6 (21%)	0 (0%)	28 (24%)
	IV	21 (62%)	11 (32%)	2 (6%)	34 (30%)
	V	4 (57%)	2 (29%)	1 (14%)	7 (6%)
		79 (69%)	32 (28%)	4 (3%)	115 (100%)
MED	I	47 (44%)	33 (31%)	26 (25%)	106 (34%)
	II	18 (48%)	16 (43%)	3 (8%)	37 (12%)
	III	48 (68%)	19 (27%)	4 (6%)	71 (23%)
	IV	33 (51%)	22 (34%)	10 (15%)	65 (21%)
	V	19 (66%)	8 (28%)	2 (7%)	29 (9%)
		165 (53%)	98 (32%)	45 (15%)	308 (100%)

Table 17
Institution-level (Major) Disciplinary Infractions by AIMS Group
(Two Institutions)

	Group	0	1 - 2	3 or more	Total by group
MIN	I	9 (32%)	14 (50%)	5 (18%)	28 (24%)
	II	9 (50%)	8 (44%)	1 (6%)	18 (16%)
	III	16 (57%)	10 (36%)	2 (7%)	28 (24%)
	IV	19 (56%)	11 (32%)	4 (12%)	34 (30%)
	V	1 (14%)	4 (57%)	2 (29%)	7 (6%)
		54 (47%)	47 (41%)	14 (12%)	115 (100%)
MED	I	36 (34%)	41 (39%)	29 (27%)	106 (34%)
	II	20 (54%)	13 (35%)	4 (11%)	37 (12%)
	III	50 (70%)	16 (23%)	5 (7%)	71 (23%)
	IV	26 (40%)	22 (34%)	17 (26%)	65 (21%)
	V	10 (34%)	11 (38%)	8 (28%)	29 (9%)
		142 (46%)	103 (33%)	63 (20%)	308 (100%)

to 34% of Group I. At the other extreme, 27% of Group I had three or more serious infractions, compared to only 7% of Group III. These results are all in the predicted direction, lending support to AIMS' construct validity.

It is of interest that Group V had proportionately greater involvement in the more serious disciplinary infractions than in the less serious. Comparing the distribution of Group V cases across the two levels of misconduct produced a X^2 of 6.86 (df = 2, p = .03). This suggests that when members of this anxious and conflicted subgroup did break institution rules, they tended to do so in relatively more serious ways—lending some credence to the underlying explosive nature of these individuals.

A more detailed analysis of the relationship between group membership and misconduct infractions involved grouping the incidents into three separate classes. The "aggressive" disciplinary reports covered six offenses (assault, fighting, threatening bodily harm, extortion, destroying property, and possession of a weapon); the "noncompliant" category encompassed five offenses (refusing to work, refusing to obey, fail-

Figure 6
Post-release Data—Total Sample

Post-release sample		
AIMS Group	N	% of total
I	67	30.5
II	24	10.9
III	60	27.3
IV	52	23.6
V	17	7.7
	220	100.0

Subsample: No record of rearrest			
Group	N	% of post-release AIMS group	% of total subsample
I	40	59.7	26.5
II	18	75.0	11.9
III	49	81.7	32.5
IV	29	55.8	19.2
V	15	88.2	9.9
	151	(% of total sample 68.63)	

Subsample: Parole violation only			
Group	N	% of post-release AIMS group	% of total subsample
I	1	1.5	50.0
II	0	0.0	—
III	1	1.6	50.0
IV	0	0.0	—
V	0	0.0	—
	2	(% of total sample 0.91)	

Subsample: Rearrested			
Group	N	% of post-release AIMS group	% of total subsample
I	26	38.8	38.8
II	6	25.0	9.0
III	10	16.7	14.9
IV	23	44.2	34.3
V	2	11.8	3.0
	67	(% of total sample 30.45)	

ing to perform work as instructed, insolence, and lying); the "other" class included possession of drugs, misuse of medication, loaning property for an increased return, possession of unauthorized goods, and possession of another's property.

An analysis of variance on the means of the five groups for aggressive infractions revealed that the groups differed significantly (F = 3.62; df = 4, 317, p = .007), with the mean of Group I significantly higher than those of Groups II and III. The groups also differed on number of noncompliance disciplinary reports (F = 6.07; df = 4, 317, p = .0001); Group I again exceeded all others, which did not differ among themselves. The groups did not differ significantly in regard to the "other" infractions.

It is clear and in line with predictions that Group I not only incurs the greatest number of disciplinary reports overall—it also receives the most severe ones as well as the highest number involving aggressiveness and noncompliance with institutional regulations.

Additional data related to group membership and inmate aggression comes from the Federal Correctional Institution at Petersburg, Virginia. On December 25, 1982, a major disturbance in the Petersburg dining room between rival inmate factions resulted in the death of a correctional officer. At the time of this tragedy the institution was already implementing AIMS in making its living unit assignments, with Heavies (Groups I & II), Moderates (Group III), and Lights (Groups IV & V) housed separately. The dining room, however, was used simultaneously by more than one living unit.

Subsequent investigation revealed that a group of 20 inmates were primarily responsible for the disturbance. Of these, 85% were Heavies (Groups I & II), while none were Moderates or Lights (Group III or Groups IV & V). (The remaining 15% were from a drug treatment unit or not yet classified.) The 85%-representation figure for Group I & II contrasts with the fact that Heavies represented only 29% of the institution's total inmate population. Inmates who were classified in the Bureau of Prisons' security-level-4 category (see Figure 4) were also overrepresented (53% in the disturbance group vs. 31% in the institution's total population), while prisoners in the lower security levels (1, 2, and 3) were underrepresented.

Post-Release Behavior

By June 1983, 220 cases in the basic random sample had been released from confinement; information as to their subsequent arrests, convictions, and incarcerations was obtained from the National Crime Information Center (NCIC) files. In order to equate all cases for post-release exposure time, a two-year "window" was chosen; a three-year post-release period would have eliminated too many subjects who had not been free that long. (It should be noted that the two-year follow-up period covers parts of different calendar years for different releasees.) Although reduction in sample size for the post-release analysis is unfortunate, the cases remaining do match the total random sample percentages within the five AIMS groups (Appendix 24).[1]

Post-release behavior was measured in a number of different ways to compensate for the fact that almost all indices of "recidivism" have some limitation. The findings relevant to the various criteria are presented in flowchart form in Figures 6, 7, and 8.

Rearrest vs. non-arrest. As can be seen in Figure 6, 151 cases (68.6%) in the follow-up sample had no recorded rearrests whatsoever. Only two releasees (1%) had rearrests solely for parole violations; presumably these were of the technical type since no other NCIC crime code was found in the file. Sixty-seven individuals (30.5%) were rearrested at least once. The number of cases in the five AIMS groups who were or were not rearrested are disproportionate; Groups I and IV had proportionately more arrests ($X^2 = 10.7$; df = 4, .05 > p > .02.

Those rearrested were further subdivided according to frequency of occurrence (single vs. multiple) and whether or not rearrest led to confinement (Figure 7). Twenty individuals (30% of the 67

> **Group III is much less involved in crime (than Group I), does not present serious management problems, and generally refrains from violence within the institution and following release.**

Figure 7
Rearrest Data by Confinement vs. Non-confinement and Frequency of Occurrence

Subsample: Rearrested
Number	67
% of post-release sample	30.45%

Subsample: Single rearrest without confinement

Group	N	% of post-release AIMS group	% of total subsample
I	4	6.0	20.0
II	2	8.3	10.0
III	4	6.6	20.0
IV	9	17.3	45.0
V	1	5.8	5.0
	20	(% of total sample 9.09)	

Subsample: Multiple rearrests without confinement

Group	N	% of post-release AIMS group	% of total subsample
I	10	14.9	62.5
II	0	0.0	—
III	1	1.6	6.3
IV	5	9.6	31.2
V	0	0.0	—
	16	(% of total sample 7.27)	

Subsample: Sentence less than one year

Group	N	% of post-release AIMS group	% of total subsample
I	2	3.0	40.0
II	2	8.3	40.0
III	1	1.6	20.0
IV	0	0.0	—
V	0	0.0	—
	5	(% of total sample 2.27)	

Subsample: Sentence more than one year

Group	N	% of post-release AIMS group	% of total subsample
I	10	14.9	38.5
II	2	8.3	7.7
III	4	6.6	15.4
IV	9	17.3	34.6
V	1	5.8	3.8
	26	(% of total sample 11.81)	

Average Sentence Length

Group	N	Total time	$\bar{x}$ time
I	10	95.20	9.52
II	2	21.00	10.50
III	4	20.50	5.12
IV	9	64.60	7.17
V	1	6.00	6.00
	26	207.30	7.97

Figure 8
Rearrest Data by Type of Crime and Frequency of Occurrence

Subsample: Rearrested
Number	67
% of post-release sample	30.45%

Subsample: Single rearrest - nonviolent crime

Group	N	% of post-release AIMS group	% of total subsample
I	8	11.9	29.6
II	2	8.3	7.4
III	6	10.0	22.2
IV	9	17.3	33.3
V	2	11.7	7.4
	27	(% of total sample	12.27)

Subsample: Single rearrest - violent crime

Group	N	% of post-release AIMS group	% of total subsample
I	5	7.5	50.0
II	1	4.1	10.0
III	0	0.0	—
IV	4	7.7	40.0
V	0	0.0	—
	10	(% of total sample	4.54)

Subsample: Multiple rearrests - nonviolent crime

Group	N	% of post-release AIMS group	% of total subsample
I	6	8.9	30.0
II	2	8.3	10.0
III	4	6.6	20.0
IV	8	15.3	40.0
V	0	0.0	—
	20	(% of total sample	9.09)

Subsample: Multiple rearrests - violent crime

Group	N	% of post-release AIMS group	% of total subsample
I	7	10.4	70.0
II	1	4.1	10.0
III	0	0.0	—
IV	2	3.8	20.0
V	0	0.0	—
	10	(% of total sample	4.54)

**Figure 9
Violent vs. Nonviolent Rearrests**

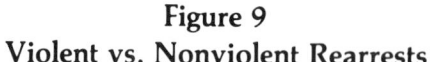

Subsample: Rearrested		
Number		67
% of post-release sample		30.45%

Subsample: Rearrested · one or more nonviolent crimes			
Group	N	% of post-release AIMS group	% of total subsample
I	14	20.9	29.8
II	4	16.6	8.5
III	10	16.6	21.3
IV	17	32.7	36.2
V	2	11.7	4.3
	47	(% of total sample	21.36)

Subsample: Rearrested · one or more violent crimes			
Group	N	% of post-release AIMS group	% of total subsample
I	12	17.9	60.0
II	2	8.3	10.0
III	0	0.0	—
IV	6	11.5	30.0
V	0	0.0	—
	20	(% of total sample	9.09)

rearrest cases; 9% of the total sample) had a record of only one rearrest. There were no significant differences on the one-arrest variable among the groups.

Sixteen cases were rearrested more than once (24% of those rearrested and 7.2% of the total sample). Again, Groups I and IV were overrepresented ($X^2 = 11.33$; df = 4, $.05 > p > .02$); these two groups account for 15 of the 16 releasees rearrested more than once but not confined.

Rearrest and confinement. Thirty-one cases (46% of those rearrested; 14% of the total sample) were sentenced to jail or prison (Figure 7). Only 5 individuals received sentences of less than one year, while 26 were sentenced to one year or longer (39% of the rearrested group; 11.8% of the total). Although Groups I and IV appear to be overrepresented among these latter cases, the discrepancy was not statistically significant ($X^2 = 4.23$; df = 4, $p > .30$).

Rearrest for violent vs. nonviolent crimes. Of the 67 releasees rearrested, 27 (40% of the 67 rearrested) experienced a single rearrest for a nonviolent crime (Figure 8). Ten individuals (15% of those rearrested) were rearrested for a single violent crime—murder, aggravated assault, forcible rape, robbery (FBI categorization). Twenty (30% of those rearrested) were rearrested for multiple nonviolent crimes, while 10 individuals (15% of those rearrested) were rearrested for multiple violent crimes.

Figure 9 combines the rearrest cases to show those rearrested for violent vs. nonviolent crimes. Twenty releasees (30% of those rearrested; 9% of the total) were rearrested for at least one violent crime, as opposed to 47 cases (70% of those rearrested; 21% of the total) who were rearrested for at least one nonviolent crime. The violent crimes were disproportionate in both Group I (100% more than expected on a statistical basis) and Group IV (50% more than expected) ($X^2 = 13.05$; df = 4, $.02 > p > .01$). Group I releasees, who represent 30.5% of the total follow-up sample, were responsible for 60% of the recorded violent offenses. Conversely, Groups III and V, representing 35% of the follow-up sample, committed no (0%) violent offenses.

Overall, the data clearly demonstrate significantly higher post-release failure rates (rearrests, confinements, violent crimes) in Groups I and IV.[2]

Summary

The available data demonstrate clear differences among the AIMS groups on a variety of variables relevant to the correctional process. Groups I and III show the greatest contrast, with Group I manifesting greater criminal involvement, poorer institutional adjustment, and a tendency toward violence both inside prison and post-release. Group III is much less involved in crime, does not present serious management problems, and generally refrains from violence within the institution and following release. Groups II and IV are in an intermediate position but, with certain exceptions, are closer to Group III than to Group I.

The relatively high post-release failure rate of Group IV was surprising; it has been suggested that this may be due to involvement with drugs and/or alcohol. Group V represented a very small part of the various study samples; there is little we can say about them at this time that truly sets them apart.

Regarding the construct validity of AIMS for classifying offenders, the data reported herein are overwhelmingly in the direction anticipated. In both their variety and magnitude, they represent strong support for the validity of the system.

> ...the data reported are overwhelmingly in the direction anticipated. In both their variety and magnitude, they represent strong support for the validity of the system.

Notes

1. A five-year follow-up of these offenders is the ultimate goal. Additional data on a two- and possibly a three-year follow-up of a large proportion of the total sample is expected to be available in 1984.

2. Megargee & Bohn (1979) have reported recidivism data on a sample of 1,011 men relased from a single federal institution serving inmates comparable to those reported on here. Their cohort had a mean time on release of 42.8 months with a range from 18 to 67 months. The overall rate of one-or-more rearrests for their group was 52% (as compared to 31% for this sample). Also, 26% were reincarcerated (Megargee & Bohn, 1979, pp. 172-173), compared to 14% in this sample.

It is of interest to note that there were no significant differences in rates of rearrest, reconviction, or reincarceration among inmates classified according to Megargee's 10 MMPI-based profile types. Differences were found among his groups on a measure rating overall post-release "success" and on the number of lines of data in the NCIC record (the latter apparently was a measure of frequency of arrest; the former included judged seriousness).

The higher failure rates in Megargee & Bohn's much larger sample may be due to a longer average follow-up period. However, as those authors point out (p. 150), the literature indicates that 85% of the releasees who recidivate do so within two years. It seems unlikely that the rates found in this present study would approach theirs were our follow-up period to be extended, particularly since some unknown percentage of their cases presumably were "on the streets" for only 18 months to two years.

REFERENCES

American Correctional Association. *Design Guide for Secure Adult Correctional Facilities.* College Park, MD: American Correctional Association, 1983.

Auffrey, J. J. "An Evaluation of the Quay Classification System at the Muskegan Correctional Facility: Preliminary Results." December 1978. (Unpublished)

Bohn, M. J., Jr. "Management Classification for Young Adult Inmates." *Federal Probation* 43 (1979): 53-59.

Bureau of Prisons. "Security Designation and Custody Classification System." Program Statement 5100.1. Washington, D.C.: Bureau of Prisons, U.S. Department of Justice, 1979. (Mimeographed)

Carkhuff, R. R. *Helping in Human Relations.* New York: Holt, Rinehart and Winston, 1969.

_____. *The Art of Helping: An Introduction to Life Skills.* Amherst, ME: Human Resource Development Press, 1973.

Fowler, M. G., & Megargee, E. I. "Psychometric Characteristics of Megargee's Work Performance and Interpersonal Adjustment Rating Schedules." *Criminal Justice and Behavior* 3 (1976): 361-370.

Gerard, R.E. "Institutional Innovations in Juvenile Corrections." *Federal Probation* 34 (1970): 37-44.

Harman, H. H. *Modern Factor Analysis.* 2nd ed., rev. Chicago: University of Chicago Press, 1970.

Levinson, R. B. "A Clarification of Classification." *Criminal Justice and Behavior* 9 (1982): 133-142.

Levinson, R. B., & Gerard, R. E. "Functional Units: A Different Correctional Approach." *Federal Probation* (December 1972).

Megargee, E. I. "Standardized Reports of Work Performance and Inmate Adjustment for Use in Correctional Settings." *Correctional Psychologist* 5 (1972): 48-54.

_____. "A New Classification System for Offenders." *Criminal Justice and Behavior* 4 (1977): 107-216.

Megargee, E. I., & Bohn, M. J., Jr. *Classifying Criminal Offenders: A New System Based on the MMPI.* Beverly Hills, CA: Sage, 1979.

National Institute of Corrections. *Prison Classification: A Model Systems Approach.* Washington, DC: National Institute of Corrections, U.S. Department of Justice, 1981. (Mimeographed)

Quay, H. C. *The Differential Behavioral Classification of the Adult Male Offender.* Technical report prepared for the Bureau of Prisons, U.S. Department of Justice (Contract J-1C-22,253). Philadelphia: Temple University, 1974.

(References, continued)

_____. "Personality and Delinquency." In *Juvenile Delinquency*. Princeton, NJ: Van Nostrand, 1965.

Quay, H. C., and Parsons, L. B. *The Differential Behavioral Classification of the Juvenile Offender.* Washington, DC: U.S. Bureau of Prisons, 1971.

Smith, W.A., & Fenton, C.E. "Unit Management in a Penitentiary: A Practical Experience." *Federal Probation* 42 (1978): 40-46.

Solomon, L. "Developing an Empirically Based Model for Classification Decision-making." *Prison Law Monitor* 2 (1980): 217, 234-237.

Warren, M. Q. "The Case for Differential Treatment of Delinquents." *Annals of the American Academy of Politics and Social Science* 381 (1969): 47-59.

APPENDIXES

1. Principles of Classification (National Institute of Corrections), 55
2. Correctional Adjustment Checklist (CACL), 61
3. Checklist for the Analysis of Life History Records of Adult Offenders (CALH), 62
4. Raw Score Form: Correctional Adjustment Checklist (CACL), 63
5. Raw Score Form: Life History Checklist (CALH), 64
6. Classification Profile for Adult Offenders, 65
7. Raw Score to Normalized T-score Conversions for Correctional Adjustment Checklist (CACL), 66
8. Raw Score to Normalized T-score Conversions for Life History Checklist (CALH), 67
9. Distribution of Subjects by Institution for Developing the Correctional Adjustment Checklist (CACL), 67
10. Rotated Factor Loadings, Correctional Adjustment Checklist (CACL), 68
11. Key for Items on Correctional Adjustment Checklist (CACL), 70
12. Raw Score Distribution for Scale I, Correctional Adjustment Checklist (CACL), 71
13. Raw Score Distribution for Scale II, Correctional Adjustment Checklist (CACL), 71
14. Raw Score Distribution for Scale IV, Correctional Adjustment Checklist (CACL), 72
15. Raw Score Distribution for Scale V, Correctional Adjustment Checklist (CACL), 72
16. Conversion of Raw Scores to Normalized T-scores for Correctional Adjustment Checklist (CACL) Scales, 73
17. Distribution of Subjects by Institution for Developing the Life History Checklist (CALH), 73
18. Rotated Factor Loadings, Life History Checklist (CALH), 74
19. Key for Items on Life History Checklist (CALH), 76
20. Raw Score Distributions for Life History Checklist (CALH) Scales, 77
21. Conversion of Raw Scores to Normalized T-scores for Life History Checklist (CALH) Scales, 78

(Appendixes, continued)

22. Sample Distribution by AIMS Group in Two Institutions (MIN and MED), 78
23. Comparison of Distribution of Cases by AIMS Group: Total Sample vs. Random Sample, 79
24. Comparison of Post-release Sample with Random Sample, 79

Appendix 1.
Principles of Classification

The foundation of classification is a *system*—the organized and established procedure for combining an interdependent group of events into a unified whole. A system entails the coming together of all components to produce a product: *classification.* The type of system that exists will determine the type of classification that exists. The *process* by which classification is effected is an integral part of the product. If the process (embodied in the policy and procedure manual) changes, then the classification decisions will change.

Any classification system must operate on the basis of valid principles; those presented below describe the factors necessary for a classification *system* to exist (Solomon, 1980). (In addition, the 14 principles listed below make up the criteria for a classification system assessment tool for evaluating basic system functioning. Specific methods for use of the principles as an assessment tool are discussed in Section 5, *Prison Classification: A Model Systems Approach*.) It is important to note that the following principles must apply to the *entire* prison system, including women and youthful offender institutions and programs.

1. **There must be a clear definition of goals and objectives of the total correctional system.**

    Traditionally, security and custody have been the primary goals and objectives of correctional systems. While most also have rehabilitation as a goal, it is secondary to security and custody, as the latter comprise the primary public mandate to corrections. Humane care and treatment, however, should be integral to all systems.

    Prior to attempting to design a classification process or other system-wide program, the Department of Corrections must be very clear as to its own goals and objectives (its function, purpose, and priorities). These should be realistic and understandable to both staff and inmates.

    Within these goals, a classification system can be developed to sort those prisoners whose identified needs fall within the agency's objectives. Only after conceptualizing its own goals can a correctional system develop a rational classification process.

2. **There must be detailed written procedures and policies governing the classification process.**

    An essential component for a classification decision-making model is a policy statement that sets forth the Department of Corrections' goals, objectives, and purposes for the new classification system. For example, when developing its new classification system in 1979, the Minnesota Department of Corrections based the system on eight departmental "principles" regarding classification. These principles, in order of importance to Minnesota's Department of Corrections, are:

    - Minimize risk to the public;

    - Minimize risk to other inmates and institution staff;

    - Minimize breaches of security;

    - Minimize system risk;

    - Minimize security levels;

    - Maximize fairness (similar offenders treated in a similar manner);

    - Maximize the objective and quantitative nature of all classification criteria; and

    - Maximize inmate understanding of the classification system and inmate participation in program decisions.

Excerpted from *Prison Classification: A Model Systems Approach,* National Institute of Corrections, U.S. Department of Justice, 1981.

Policies such as Minnesota's should be included in a comprehensive departmental classification policy manual. The American Correctional Association (ACA) *Manual of Standards for Adult Correctional Institutions* (1977) calls "essential" (Standard No. 4373) a "... classification manual containing all the classification policies and detailed procedures for implementing policies; this manual is made available to all staff involved with classification and is reviewed at least annually and updated as necessary."* The manual must be written clearly and concisely, and *must* be understood by classification personnel. The policies contained in the manual should deal with such classification issues as:

- Initial inmate classification and reclassification;

- Instructions regarding the makeup of classification committees, units, and teams, and the full responsibilities of each;

- Definitions of various committees' responsibilities for custody, employment, and vocational/program assignments;

- Instructions concerning potential changes in an inmate's program;

- Procedures relating to inmate transfer from one program to another and from one institution to another;

- Content of the classification interview; and

- Method of documentation of decisions made.

Since classification policies must be dynamic, constantly subject to change and revision as the classification process is continuously evaluated, the classification manual should be prepared in such a manner as to provide for easy update. (An important caution here is that the length of the manual is not necessarily correlated with its quality.)

3. **The classification process must provide for the collection of complete, high-quality, verified, standardized data.**

    The classification system must define the data needed and the format in which it is to be collected and analyzed. High-quality, standardized data is essential to a valid statistical base for classification decision-making and for correlation of prediction and need factors.

    Complete and verified data permits:

    - Equitable determinations based on particular factors of individual cases;

    - Similar decisions among individual classification analysts on roughly comparable cases; and

    - Quantitative analysis of trends in classification decision-making for individual facilities or the Department of Corrections as a whole.

    Through its technical assistance projects, NIC has found that the quantity and quality of offender data (criminal history, personal and family background, etc.) available to teams when the classification decision must be made are frequently less than adequate, and sometimes entirely unusable. Forms often are incomplete, some data collected are of questionable relevance, and much information is subject to broad interpretation because of its qualitative (narrative) nature.

---

*This standard has since been superseded by Standard 2-4399, which states: "There is a written plan for inmate classification which specifies the objectives of the classification system, details the methods for achieving the objectives, and provides a monitoring and evaluation mechanism to determine whether the objectives are being met. The plan is reviewed at least annually and updated if necessary." *Standards for Adult Correctional Institutions,* Second Edition, 1981.

In many of the systems studied, NIC found that no specific guidelines were given to field staff regarding the collection of offender background data necessary for a valid classification decision. Without specific and objective guidelines, field staff are not likely to prepare reports sufficiently comprehensive and reliable to be used in an empirically valid statistical analysis.

4. **Measurement and testing instruments used in the classification decision-making process must be valid, reliable, and objective.**

The numerous legal grievances filed by prisoners in recent years charging that classification decision-making processes are discriminatory, biased, or invalid, point up the necessity to ensure that any tests administered to inmates have been validated for reliability as predictors of custody and/or program needs. In addition, correctional departments must be able to demonstrate that testing processes are objective, logical, and fundamentally fair, and are designed to meet the needs of both the prisoners and the institution. By the same token, tests designed for other purposes should not be used to classify inmates (I.Q. tests, personality inventories).

In mid-1979, NIC sponsored a national survey of screening and classification processes, which assessed the current state-of-the-art in the design and utilization of classification instruments for decision-making (American Justice Institute, 1979). The survey found that correctional agencies have been shifting from subjective judgments to standardized instruments for classification decision-making. The instruments being used are printed forms containing a fixed set of weighted criteria that provide an overall offender summary score. Considerations of this score in the process assists the classification team in making more uniform and consistent decisions that are less subject to legal challenge. (North Carolina and Minnesota submitted their instruments for legal review prior to implementation.) In some states, the forms are used both for custody and needs decision-making.

5. **There must be explicit policy statements structuring and checking the discretionary decision-making powers of classification team staff.**

A corrections department must establish clear guidelines governing the discretionary decision-making powers of classification team staff. Otherwise, the department leaves itself open to allegations of unfairness, arbitrariness, and bias.

Discretionary powers of classification staff remain unstructured in too many systems. One example of the resultant problems was provided by a state corrections department in a grant application to NIC: "There is a very broad range of subjective and informal criteria used by those responsible for the classification of inmates; each person involved in the classification process has internalized his own set of significant variables, has established the relative importance of each of these variables according to his own value scale, and applies these standards in the classification decision on a case-by-case basis."

While discretion cannot and should not be completely eliminated, steps can be taken to designate boundaries within which classification decisions will be made, thus eliminating too broad discretionary power of individuals. A system in which the classification processes, rules, policies, findings, and reasons are open to scrutiny can further serve to check discretion.

Structuring and checking discretion is the responsibility of the Department of Corrections' central office. This responsibility is carried out by:

- Direction and supervision of the classification process by high-level central office personnel;

- Establishment of procedures for inter-institutional transfer, including review by central office staff and an appeal procedure and administrative review of difficult cases;

- Establishment of procedures for central office monitoring and evaluation of the classification process to ensure that it is operating according to policy;

- Establishment of procedures for consideration of mitigating or aggravating factors in decision-making;

- Initiation of policy pertaining to classification, inmate programs/treatment, and casework, including a classification manual; and

- Selection, training, and supervision of counselors and other classification staff members.

6. **There must be provision for screening and further evaluating prisoners who are management problems and those who have special needs.**

    This necessary function, also the responsibility of the Department of Corrections' central office, must be included in any model classification system.

    Prisoners who are management problems and require special considerations in placement and programming fall into several categories:

    - Those who require protection and separation because they may be in danger from other prisoners;

    - Those who, by reason of their offense, criminal record, or institutional behavior, require particularly close supervision; and

    - Those who received unusual publicity because of the nature of their crime, arrest, or trial, or who were involved in criminal activities of a sophisticated nature, such as organized crime.

    The most dangerous inmates must be separated from the less violent individuals; thus, the classification process, by necessity, needs to include procedures to determine which prisoners are potentially dangerous, such as those who have a history of assaultive or predatory behavior.

    In additon to screening and further evaluating inmates who are management problems, the correctional system's central office must provide for prisoners who have special needs. Those individuals who, through effective screening, are shown to require special program assignments and monitoring include, but are not limited to, the aged and infirm, the mentally ill and retarded, and those with special medical problems.

7. **There must be provisions to match offenders with programs; these provisions must be consistent with risk classification needs.**

    This process involves the establishment of clear, operational definitions of the various types of offenders and available institutional programs. But risk as well as need factors must be considered when decisions are being made.

    Thus, NIC recommends that the classification process be directed toward:

    - Identifying and evaluating the factors underlying each prisoner's needs;

    - Recommending programs and activities for prisoners according to their *specific* needs and the availability of resources; and

    - Developing and recording the necessary data to support services and long-range program planning.

    To fulfill these tasks, it is necessary to identify and utilize *all* programs that are available to each individual prisoner. This function can be accomplished through a systematic classification of the offender and subsequent development of a program plan specifically designed for him/her.

8. **There must be provisions to classify each prisoner at the least restrictive custody level.**

    This model classification system component targets the prevalent problem of overclassification. Eliminating overclassification is among the most significant objectives of new classification systems being designed and implemented in Minnesota, Tennessee, New York, and other states.

The first step involved here is developing specific criteria for differential custody assignments. Equally crucial is the second step of ensuring that both staff and prisoners are aware of these criteria.

NIC recommends that clearly understandable custody definitions and supervision guidelines be applied system-wide. At a minimum, definitions should be given for: (1) the traditional levels of custody — maximum, close, medium, and community; and (2) the different uses of segregation (especially disciplinary segregation). A basic premise is that *every* prisoner should be in the *lowest* custody believed suitable for adequate supervision and warranted by his/her behavior.

9. There must be provision to involve the prisoner in the classification process.

Each new prisoner should be provided with a copy of the custody criteria; a written explanation of the classification process; and a written explanation of the health care, employment, vocational training, education, transfer, and special programs available, including the selection criteria for each.

In addition, the correctional system should provide for classification teams at each institution so the prisoner can participate in the classification decision-making process. ACA Standard No. 4374 [Standard 2-4403, Second Edition, 1981] calls for "maximum involvement of inmates in their classification reviews." The prisoner should be present except, perhaps, during deliberations of the classification team.

10. There must be provisions for systematic, periodic reclassification hearings.

Providing for reclassification on a regularly scheduled basis is another "essential" standard (No. 4376) [Standard 2-4404, Second Edition, 1981] recommended by the ACA. Periodic review and reclassification is a cornerstone of any model classification system.

In reporting on its study of the classification process at the Tennessee Department of Corrections, NIC suggested the adoption of the following reclassification guidelines:

- Review/reclassification within two weeks following the prisoner's transfer from another institution within the system;

- Review every three months for prisoners serving terms of 18 months or less;

- Review every six months for prisoners serving terms of 18 months and one day to five years; and

- Annual review for prisoners serving terms of five years or more. (NIC now recommends review every six months.)

If suitable manpower is available, reviews can be conducted on a more frequent basis. Optimally, prisoners should be permitted to initiate reviews of their progress, status, and programming (ACA "important" Standard No. 4379) [Standard 2-4407, Second Edition, 1981].

11. The classification process must be efficient and economically sound.

An empirically based classification system should enable the Department of Corrections to handle large numbers of offenders efficiently through a grouping process based on needs and risks. This can be accomplished by using modern technology to assist in the storage, correlation, and retrieval of data, although use of a computer should not be essential.

An efficient, economically sound classification system also makes effective use of other components of the criminal justice system, as well as social service agencies, for the provision of offender data (such as information obtained for pre-sentence reports).

The development of a model classification system should involve cooperating with other agencies to devise a standardized reporting format for offender information, preferably one which elicits quantitative data insofar as possible.

12. **There must be provisions to continuously evaluate and improve the classification process.**

    Any true process continuously strives to improve itself through feedback, evaluation, and action to correct deficiencies. Thus, the model classification system, if it is to be effective, must be able to continuously improve to meet the changing needs of the inmate population and the correctional system as a whole. It must be responsive to emerging knowledge and professional understanding of the classification process. The system must also be responsive to staff and inmate input.

13. **Classification procedures must be consistent with constitutional requisites.**

    The central office must keep abreast of litigation applicable to its jurisdiction in order to ensure the continued legality of its classification policies, procedures, and decisions. Most state Departments of Corrections have a legal section that can be of assistance in this area.

14. **There must be an opportunity to gain input from administration and line staff when undertaking development of a classification system.**

In summary, *the hallmark of classification is the non-capricious assignment of individuals.* In order to accomplish equity in custody, security, program and treatment determination, and placement, a system reflecting the above principles must exist. Furthermore, it must be utilized.

A basic tenet of classification takes the idea of non-capricious placement a step further. As stated earlier, classification seeks to determine the placement of individuals in accord with their various correctional needs. Each of these outcomes may be accomplished separately, but it is only when they are combined into a comprehensive process that strives for equity and objectivity that we define it as *classification.* Since equity and objectivity are goals, principles and procedures should be employed that reflect these aims.

Appendix 2.
Correctional Adjustment Checklist (CACL)

Name and number of inmate _____
Name of person completing this checklist _____
Your position _____ Date completed _____

Instructions: Please indicate which of the following behaviors this inmate exhibits. If the behavior describes the inmate, circle the "1." If it does not, circle the "0." *Please complete every item.*

0	1	1. Worried, anxious
0	1	2. Tries, but cannot seem to follow directions
0	1	3. Tense, unable to relax
0	1	4. Socially withdrawn
0	1	5. Continually asks for help from staff
0	1	6. Gets along with the hoods
0	1	7. Seems to take no pleasure in anything
0	1	8. Jittery, jumpy; seems afraid
0	1	9. Uses leisure time to cause trouble
0	1	10. Continually uses profane language; curses and swears
0	1	11. Easily upset
0	1	12. Sluggish and drowsy
0	1	13. Cannot be trusted at all
0	1	14. Moody, brooding
0	1	15. Needs constant supervision
0	1	16. Victimizes weaker inmates
0	1	17. Seems dull and unintelligent
0	1	18. Is an agitator about race
0	1	19. Continually tries to con staff
0	1	20. Impulsive; unpredictable
0	1	21. Afraid of other inmates
0	1	22. Seems to seek excitement
0	1	23. Never seems happy
0	1	24. Doesn't trust staff
0	1	25. Passive; easily led
0	1	26. Talks aggressively to other inmates
0	1	27. Accepts no blame for any of his troubles
0	1	28. Continually complains; accuses staff of unfairness
0	1	29. Daydreams; seems to be mentally off in space
0	1	30. Talks aggressively to staff
0	1	31. Has a quick temper
0	1	32. Obviously holds grudges; seeks to "get even"
0	1	33. Inattentive; seems preoccupied
0	1	34. Attempts to play staff against one another
0	1	35. Passively resistant; has to be forced to participate
0	1	36. Tries to form a clique
0	1	37. Openly defies regulations and rules
0	1	38. Often sad and depressed
0	1	39. Stirs up trouble among inmates
0	1	40. Aids or abets others in breaking the rules
0	1	41. Considers himself unjustly confined

Source: Herbert C. Quay, Ph.D.

Appendix 3.
Checklist for the Analysis of Life History Records of Adult Offenders (CALH)

Name and number of inmate _____
Name of person completing this checklist _____
Your position _____ Date completed _____

Instructions: Place a checkmark before each behavior trait that describes this inmate's life history.

_____ 1. Has few, if any, friends
_____ 2. Thrill-seeking
_____ 3. Preoccupied; "dreamy"
_____ 4. Uncontrollable as a child
_____ 5. Has expressed guilt over offense
_____ 6. Expresses need for self-improvement
_____ 7. Socially withdrawn
_____ 8. Weak, indecisive, easily led
_____ 9. Previous local, state, or federal incarceration
_____ 10. Tough, defiant
_____ 11. Irregular work history (if not a student)
_____ 12. Noted not to be responsive to counseling
_____ 13. Gives impression of ineptness, incompetence in managing everyday problems in living
_____ 14. Supported wife and children
_____ 15. Claims offense was motivated by family problems
_____ 16. Close ties with criminal elements
_____ 17. Depressed, morose
_____ 18. Physically aggressive (strong arm, assault, reckless homicide, attempted murder, mugging, etc.)
_____ 19. Apprehension likely due to "stupid" behavior on the part of the offender
_____ 20. Single marriage
_____ 21. Expresses feelings of inadequacy, worthlessness
_____ 22. Difficulties in the public schools
_____ 23. Suffered financial reverses prior to commission of offense for which incarcerated
_____ 24. Passive, submissive
_____ 25. Bravado, braggart
_____ 26. Guiltless; blames others
_____ 27. Expresses lack of concern for others

Source: Herbert C. Quay, Ph.D.

Appendix 4.
Raw Score Form: Correctional Adjustment Checklist (CACL)

Name and number of inmate _____
Name of person completing this checklist _____
Your position _____ Date completed _____

Instructions: For each "1" circled on the Correctional Adjustment Checklist, place a checkmark on the line corresponding to the item number. Add the checkmarks to obtain the Raw Score for each group.

Group

I	II	IV	V
			1. _____
		2. _____	3. _____
		4. _____	5. _____
6. _____		7. _____	8. _____
9. _____			
10. _____			11. _____
		12. _____	
13. _____		14. _____	
15. _____			
16. _____		17. _____	
18. _____	19. _____		
20. _____			21. _____
22. _____		23. _____	
	24. _____	25. _____	
26. _____			
27. _____	28. _____	29. _____	
30. _____			
31. _____			
32. _____		33. _____	
	34. _____	35. _____	
36. _____			
37. _____			38. _____
39. _____			
40. _____	41. _____		
Total (Raw Score) _____	_____	_____	_____

Source: Herbert C. Quay, Ph.D.

Appendix 5.
Raw Score Form: Life History Checklist (CALH)

Name and number of inmate _____

Name of person completing this checklist _____

Your position _____ Date completed _____

Instructions: For each item checked on the Checklist for the Analysis of Life History Records of Adult Offenders, place a checkmark on the line corresponding to the item number. Add the checkmarks to obtain the Raw Score for each group.

Group

I	III	IV
		1. ____
2. ____		3. ____
4. ____		
	5. ____	
	6. ____	
		7. ____
		8. ____
9. ____		
10. ____		
11. ____		
12. ____		13. ____
	14. ____	
	15. ____	
16. ____		17. ____
18. ____		19. ____
	20. ____	
		21. ____
22. ____	23. ____	
		24. ____
25. ____		
26. ____		
27. ____		

Total (Raw Score) _____   _____   _____

Source: Herbert C. Quay, Ph.D.

Appendix 6.
Classification Profile for Adult Offenders

Name and number of inmate _____
Name of person completing this profile _____
Your position _____ Date completed _____

	Scale	Raw score	T-score
1. **Correctional Adjustment Checklist (CACL)**	I	_____	_____
	II	_____	_____
	IV	_____	_____
	V	_____	_____
Checklist for the Analysis of Life History Records (CALH)	I	_____	_____
	III	_____	_____
	IV	_____	_____

2. **Combined Scores**	Scale	CACL T-score	CALH T-score	Final T-score
	I	_____ +	_____ ÷ 2 =	_____
	II		_____ =	_____
	III		_____ =	_____
	IV	_____ +	_____ ÷ 2 =	_____
	V		_____ =	_____

3. **Assignment**   ___ Group I   ___ Group III   ___ Group IV
                    ___ Group II   ___ Group V

Instructions:
1. Transfer Totals from Raw Score Forms onto appropriate Raw Score lines.
   Using the appropriate conversion table, convert each Raw Score to a T-score.
   - If two CACLs are used per inmate, convert all Raw scores to T-scores; then add the T-scores obtained for each scale and divide the sum by 2.
2. List the final CACL and CALH T-scores on the appropriate lines in the Combined Scores section.
   - For Scales I and IV, add the T-scores and divide by 2.
3. Use the highest Final T-score to make the final assignment.
   If two scores are tied, use the following tie-breaker rules:
   - If Group I and Group II are tied for highest,
     —and there is one housing unit for *both* groups, assign to Heavy.
     —and there is one housing unit for *each* group, assign for the best balance or use of available housing.
   - If Group IV and Group V are tied for highest,
     —and there is one housing unit for *both* groups, assign to Light.
     —and there is one housing unit for *each* group, assign for the best balance or use of available housing.
   - If Group I *or* Group II are tied with any other group, assign to Heavy.
   - If Group IV *or* Group V are tied with Group III, assign to Light.

(**Note:** Before using any tie-breaker rules, recheck all scoring and calculations.)

Appendix 7.
Raw Score to Normalized T-score Conversions for Correctional Adjustment Checklist (CACL)

Scale I		Scale II		Scale IV		Scale V	
Raw score	T-score	Raw score	T-score	Raw score	T-score	Raw score	T-score
0	41	0	44	0	40	0	39
1	49	1	54	1	47	1	46
2	53	2	59	2	51	2	50
3	56	3	62	3	54	3	54
4	58	4	65	4	56	4	57
5	59	5	70	5	59	5	61
6	60			6	61	6	65
7	61			7	63	7	71
8	62			8	65		
9	63			9	69		
10	64			10	73		
11	65			11	78		
12	66						
13	67						
14	68						
15	69						
16	71						
17	73						
18	76						

Appendix 8.
Raw Score to Normalized T-score Conversions for Life History Checklist (CALH)

Scale I		Scale III		Scale IV	
Raw score	T-score	Raw score	T-score	Raw score	T-score
0	35	0	39	0	39
1	43	1	47	1	47
2	47	2	52	2	53
3	51	3	58	3	58
4	55	4	64	4	62
5	58	5	70	5	66
6	61	6	76	6	70
7	64			7	74
8	67			8	82
9	71			9	90
10	75				
11	82				

Appendix 9.
Distribution of Subjects by Institution for Developing the Correctional Adjustment Checklist (CACL)

Security level*	Facility	Sample A	Sample B	Sample C	Total
5	Atlanta	45	—	—	45
4	El Reno	146	82	—	228
5	Lewisburg	12	17	53	82
5	Lompoc	241	—	—	241
6	Marion	22	—	6	22
5	McNeil Is.	—	78	—	78
3	Milan	—	—	65	65
3	Petersburg	—	—	58	58
1	Seagoville	144	187	—	331
2	Tallahassee	—	49	—	49
5	Terre Haute	—	170	70	240
		610	583	246	1,439

*1 = Minimum; 6 = Maximum

Appendix 10.
Rotated Factor Loadings, Correctional Adjustment Checklist (CACL)
(decimals omitted)

Item	Sample A				Sample B			Sample C			
	I	II	IV	V	I	IV	V	I	II	IV	V
1. Worried, anxious	07	−10	16	63	14	09	−67	00	−16	−31	−62
2. Tries, but cannot seem to follow directions	−15	21	−35	63				−16	−17	−04	−37
3. Tense, unable to relax	−06	−03	−12	49	−07	−18	−62	−04	00	−50	63
4. Verbalizes values related to organized crime	−41	46	05	−15	−49	−02	−02	−28	−24	−23	02
5. Socially withdrawn*					−20	−59	−08	−28	−06	−49	−14
6. Continually asks for help from staff	03	20	06	39	−06	−01	−14	09	−08	−03	−40
7. Seeks help from other inmates	−13	24	03	13	−30	03	06	−19	−01	−17	−12
8. Gets along with the hoods	−30	39	13	−21	−51	19	05	−32	−10	−10	13
9. Seems to take no pleasure in anything*					−17	−55	−19	−26	00	−53	−23
10. Jittery, jumpy; seems afraid*					10	−23	−67	−04	14	−51	−59
11. Uses leisure time to cause trouble	−68	11	−12	−09				−77	−06	−16	04
12. Continually uses profane language	−42	27	00	−05				−43	−05	−07	−17
13. Easily upset*					−15	−12	−70	−33	−21	−23	−61
14. Sluggish and drowsy	03	12	−52	06	−05	−59	−19	−05	04	−48	−08
15. Cannot be trusted at all	−38	47	−21	−11				−51	−24	−25	−11
16. Moody, brooding*					−08	−47	−49	−15	−07	−52	−36
17. Acts tough but backs down when confronted	35	19	04	−02				−24	−31	−12	−11
18. Needs constant supervision	−36	35	−33	−17	−63	−25	−08	−46	−12	−30	−25
19. Victimizes weaker inmates	−64	20	13	−05				−74	−03	−04	05
20. Seems dull and unintelligent*					−15	−59	04	−03	−10	−48	−04
21. (Dropped)											
22. Is an agitator about race	−44	25	−02	−08				−61	−22	−03	−06
23. (Dropped)											
24. Continually tries to con staff	−28	57	05	13	−62	−03	−06	−21	−70	05	−18
25. Impulsive, unpredictable	−30	40	−19	04	−49	−20	−35	−50	−24	−24	−28
26. Afraid of other inmates*					15	−16	−42				
27. Seems to seek excitement*					−47	17	00	−46	−23	04	−10
28. Never seems happy*					−10	−61	−13	−05	−09	−67	−07
29. (Dropped)											
30. Doesn't trust staff	−27	54	−05	−03	−59	−15	02	−42	−27	−26	02

*Items not appearing on the initial CACL.

Appendix 10.
(continued)

Item	Sample A				Sample B			Sample C			
	I	II	IV	V	I	IV	V	I	II	IV	V
31. Lies to protect himself	−36	51	−10	−05	−06	−01	08	−48	−44	−12	−14
32. Purposely does not do as told	−46	29	−28	−16				−04	05	−53	−38
33. Passive, easily led*					14	−30	−22				
34. Afraid of staff	−08	29	−28	−16							
35. Speaks of crime as a way of life (sees self as professional criminal)	−46	48	03	48				−37	−21	−20	09
36. Talks aggressively to other inmates	−53	27	16	−07				−67	00	−10	−07
37. Expresses guilt for what he has done	05	−27	07	08	52	07	−08	28	12	12	03
38. Accepts no blame for any of his troubles	−12	61	−14	−03	−56	−16	04	−42	−20	−25	01
39. Continually complains, accuses staff of unfairness	−40	48	−19	48				−51	−52	−09	−15
40. Has a reputation as a big-time hood among other inmates	−54	24	25	−02							
41. Gambles	−34	35	04	08	−67	−20	−16	−07	−03	06	03
42. Daydreams, seems to be mentally off in space	05	07	−55	25	−30	08	03	02	10	−62	−03
43. Doesn't want to be a part of the system; rejects society	−29	46	−25	08	−26	17	02	−39	−05	−33	−04
44. Lacks self-confidence*					−09	−62	−11	02	00	−48	−38
45. Talks aggressively to staff	−48	29	05	04				−55	−38	03	−11
46. Cannot be given responsibility	−25	39	−45	−16				−53	−14	−30	−06
47. Has a quick temper	−40	37	−12	12	−66	−29	−10	−46	−29	00	−18
48. Obviously holds grudges, seeks to get even	−58	35	−09	15				−49	−33	−38	−04
49. Inattentive, seems preoccupied	−03	−01	−50	14	11	−42	−24	02	06	−59	12
50. Puts forth as little effort as possible	−26	32	−49	−20	−63	−02	−21	−51	−07	−27	−08
51. Attempts to play staff against one another	−33	53	−02	27				−18	−73	03	−06
52. Passively resistant, has to be forced to participate	−15	18	−34	−13	−56	−35	−05	−26	−02	−37	−13
53. Tries to form a clique	−64	25	10	−5				−70	−07	05	−05
54. Openly defies regulations and rules	−57	30	−25	−04				−71	−23	−09	05
55. Often sad and depressed	07	05	−32	40	−40	02	−43	14	00	−64	−30
56. Stirs up trouble among inmates	−68	00	−07	09				−87	−09	04	03
57. Aiding or abetting others in breaking the rules	−79	10	−02	02				−83	−21	−08	00
58. Considers himself unjustly confined	−19	55	−10	06	−64	−16	−31	−31	−51	−02	−06
59. Negative influence on other inmates	−40	11	−11	08	−14	47	07	−57	−11	−34	−01

*Items not appearing on the initial CACL.

Appendix 11.
Key for Items on Correctional Adjustment Checklist (CACL)

Scale	Item
V	1. Worried, anxious
IV	2. Tries, but cannot seem to follow directions
V	3. Tense, unable to relax
IV	4. Socially withdrawn
V	5. Continually asks for help from staff
I	6. Gets along with the hoods
IV	7. Seems to take no pleasure in anything
V	8. Jittery, jumpy; seems afraid
I	9. Uses leisure time to cause trouble
I	10. Continually uses profane language; curses and swears
V	11. Easily upset
IV	12. Sluggish and drowsy
I	13. Cannot be trusted at all
IV	14. Moody, brooding
I	15. Needs constant supervision
I	16. Victimizes weaker inmates
IV	17. Seems dull and unintelligent
I	18. Is an agitator about race
II	19. Continually tries to con staff
I	20. Impulsive; unpredictable
V	21. Afraid of other inmates
I	22. Seems to seek excitement
IV	23. Never seems happy
II	24. Doesn't trust staff
IV	25. Passive; easily led
I	26. Talks aggressively to other inmates
I	27. Accepts no blame for any of his troubles
II	28. Continually complains; accuses staff of unfairness
IV	29. Daydreams; seems to be mentally off in space
I	30. Talks aggressively to staff
I	31. Has a quick temper
I	32. Obviously holds grudges; seeks to "get even"
IV	33. Inattentive; seems preoccupied
II	34. Attempts to play staff against one another
IV	35. Passively resistant; has to be forced to participate
I	36. Tries to form a clique
I	37. Openly defies regulations and rules
V	38. Often sad and depressed
I	39. Stirs up trouble among inmates
I	40. Aids or abets others in breaking the rules
II	41. Considers himself unjustly confined

Source: Herbert C. Quay, Ph.D.

Appendix 12.
Raw Score Distribution for Scale I, Correctional Adjustment Checklist (CACL)

Raw Score	N	%	Raw Score	N	%
0	292	35.2	11	10	1.2
1	172	20.7	12	12	1.4
2	100	12.1	13	5	0.6
3	60	7.2	14	6	0.7
4	34	4.1	15	9	1.1
5	31	3.7			
			16	8	1.0
6	18	2.2	17	4	0.5
7	17	2.1	18	8	1.0
8	17	2.1			
9	9	1.1			
10	17	2.1			

Mean = 2.817
SD = 4.058
Median = 1.212
Mode = 0.000
Range = 0–18
N = 829

Appendix 13.
Raw Score Distribution for Scale II, Correctional Adjustment Checklist (CACL)

Raw Score	N	%
0	464	56.0
1	164	19.8
2	77	9.3
3	52	6.3
4	37	4.5
5	35	4.2

Mean = 0.961
SD = 1.408
Median = 0.393
Mode = 0.000
Range = 0–5
N = 829

Appendix 14.
Raw Score Distribution for Scale IV, Correctional Adjustment Checklist (CACL)

Raw Score	N	%
0	249	30.0
1	164	19.8
2	99	11.9
3	72	8.7
4	61	7.4
5	49	5.9
6	42	5.1
7	24	2.9
8	30	3.6
9	26	3.1
10	8	1.0
11	5	0.6

Mean = 2.52
SD = 2.74
Median = 1.51
Mode = 0.00
Range = 0–11
N = 829

Appendix 15.
Raw Score Distribution for Scale V, Correctional Adjustment Checklist (CACL)

Raw Score	N	%
0	208	25.1
1	151	18.2
2	124	15.0
3	90	10.9
4	102	12.2
5	74	8.9
6	51	6.2
7	29	3.5

Mean = 2.36
SD = 2.08
Median = 1.95
Mode = 0.00
Range = 0–7
N = 829

Appendix 16.
Conversion of Raw Scores to Normalized T-scores for Correctional Adjustment Checklist (CACL) Scales

Raw Scores	Normalized T-Scores			
	Scale I	Scale II	Scale IV	Scale V
0	41	44	40	39
1	49	54	47	46
2	53	59	51	50
3	56	62	54	54
4	58	65	56	57
5	59	70	59	61
6	60		61	65
7	61		63	71
8	62		65	
9	63		69	
10	64		73	
11	65		78	
12	66			
13	67			
14	68			
15	69			
16	71			
17	73			
18	76			

Appendix 17.
Distribution of Subjects by Institution for Developing the Life History Checklist (CALH)

Security level*	Facility	Sample A	Sample B	Total
4	El Reno	265	102	367
5	Lewisburg	153	—	153
5	Lompoc	495	—	495
6	Marion	32	—	32
5	McNeil Is.	—	116	116
1	Seagoville	231	224	455
2	Tallahassee	—	47	47
2	Terminal Is.	365	—	365
5	Terre Haute	—	201	201
		1,541	690	2,231

*1 = Minimum; 6 = Maximum

Appendix 18.
Rotated Factor Loadings, Life History Checklist (CALH)
(decimals omitted)

Item	Sample A			Sample B		
	I	III	IV	I	III	IV
Has few, if any, friends	10	19	37	17	−01	33
Openly verbalizes values and opinions in line with crime as a career	—	—	—	33	01	−06
Sexual deviance	—	—	—	—	—	—
Thrill seeking	48	−03	18	30	−09	13
Preoccupied, dreamy	−03	05	31	−04	02	33
Rapid mood changes	38	−07	28	25	04	30
Psychiatric diagnosis of some form of neurosis	12	−01	29	—	—	—
Uncontrollable as a child	48	23	08	42	−19	29
Has expressed guilt over offense	−17	48	16	—	51	−09
Expressed need for self-improvement	−08	36	20	—	12	05
Discharge from military service other than honorable	−02	03	07	11	−03	04
Common-law relationships with women	18	03	−02	21	06	02
Has seriously attempted suicide	—	—	—	—	—	—
Use of alcohol related to "binges" rather than everyday indulgence	16	−16	13	—	—	—
Was juvenile gang member	—	—	—	—	—	—
Boxes or wrestles as recreation	—	—	—	—	—	—
Socially withdrawn	00	13	45	−01	−10	40
Weak, indecisive, easily led	00	03	51	−16	−15	42
Previous local, state or federal incarceration	23	18	03	47	11	25
Multiple marriages	−07	−02	−09	14	18	04
Tough, defiant	55	10	−10	48	−01	−06
Irregular work history (if not a student)	27	24	18	31	−18	32
Offenses always or almost always involve others	37	−01	06	12	−02	−03
Noted not to be responsive to counseling	46	23	10	40	−13	24
Claims apprehension due to being sold out by someone else	—	—	—	—	—	—
Gives impression of ineptness, incompetence in managing everyday problems in living	21	09	51	20	−06	51
Supported wife and children	−11	53	−18	−29	54	−14
Claims offense motivated by family problems	03	46	09	−10	24	08
Unmarried	13	−48	28	01	−64	10
Impulsive	28	09	28	29	−08	37
Close ties with criminal elements	48	−05	−04	42	03	−09
Selling or smuggling narcotics	−09	−04	−15	−26	−14	−22
Conflict with wife, parents or both	15	−10	20	—	—	—
Has assaulted law officers or other official personnel	—	—	—	—	—	—
Depressed; morose	−06	−03	38	−17	14	30

Appendix 18.
(continued)

Item	Sample A			Sample B		
	I	III	IV	I	III	IV
Anxious, fearful	−02	−09	38	−04	06	28
Physically aggressive	40	12	−13	43	00	−06
Verbalized philosophical justification for offense	11	03	04	—	—	—
Involved with organized racketeering	—	—	—	—	—	—
Apprehension likely due to "stupid" behavior on part of offender	06	−13	31	−09	09	21
Excessive gambling	—	—	—	—	—	—
Single marriage	−11	37	−17	−19	45	−08
Expresses feelings of inadequacy, worthlessness	03	−02	53	−08	−01	34
Rejected for military service on moral grounds	—	—	—	—	—	—
Psychiatric diagnosis of psychopathy or sociopathy	—	—	—	—	—	—
Claims greater academic or work achievement than can be verified	—	—	—	—	—	—
Difficulties in the public school	36	16	21	35	−16	32
Escape from custody	17	14	14	22	−02	27
Suffered financial reverses prior to commission of offense	00	49	07	−11	23	01
Pushes drugs but is not a user	—	—	—	—	—	—
History of excessive use of alcohol	04	−07	10	08	17	18
Passive, submissive	−17	−02	42	−27	−18	24
Deliberate use of alias	—	—	—	—	—	—
Bravado; braggart	50	06	−01	—	—	—
Involved in confidence schemes	—	—	—	—	—	—
Guiltless, blames others	24	04	−07	34	−01	−05
Flight to avoid prosecution	10	07	01	—	—	—
Stable family life in childhood and youth	−24	−13	−03	−45	12	−28
No significant relationships with women	11	27	32	−05	−42	19
Economically dependent on others	23	14	29	—	—	—
Lived a nomadic "hippie" existence prior to offense	—	—	—	09	−13	21
Sees self in the rackets as a career	—	—	—	—	—	—
Threatens law enforcement officials	—	—	—	—	—	—
Expresses lack of concern for others	48	13	11	53	−03	−04
Frequent moves from state to state	08	05	14	18	00	20
Raised in urban slum area	28	−06	00	26	−03	−08
History of drug abuse or addiction	06	08	04	01	−24	00

Appendix 19.
Key for Items on Life History Checklist (CALH)

Scale	Item
IV	1. Has few, if any, friends
I	2. Thrill-seeking
IV	3. Preoccupied; "dreamy"
I	4. Uncontrollable as a child
III	5. Has expressed guilt over offense
III	6. Expresses need for self-improvement
IV	7. Socially withdrawn
IV	8. Weak, indecisive, easily led
I	9. Previous local, state, or federal incarceration
I	10. Tough, defiant
I	11. Irregular work history (if not a student)
I	12. Noted not to be responsive to counseling
IV	13. Gives impression of ineptness, incompetence in managing everyday problems in living
III	14. Supported wife and children
III	15. Claims offense was motivated by family problems
I	16. Close ties with criminal elements
IV	17. Depressed, morose
I	18. Physically aggressive (strong arm, assault, reckless homicide, attempted murder, mugging, etc.)
IV	19. Apprehension likely due to "stupid" behavior on the part of the offender
III	20. Single marriage
IV	21. Expresses feelings of inadequacy, worthlessness
I	22. Difficulties in the public schools
III	23. Suffered financial reverses prior to commission of offense for which incarcerated
IV	24. Passive, submissive
I	25. Bravado, braggart
I	26. Guiltless; blames others
I	27. Expresses lack of concern for others

Source: Herbert C. Quay, Ph.D.

Appendix 20.
Raw Score Distributions for Life History Checklist (CALH) Scales

Scale I

Raw Score	N	%
0	94	13.6
1	128	18.5
2	104	15.1
3	103	14.9
4	91	13.2
5	55	8.0
6	47	6.8
7	29	4.2
8	20	2.9
9	12	1.7
10	6	0.9
11	2	0.3

Mean = 3.067
SD = 2.411
Median = 2.689
Mode = 1.00
Range = 0–11
N = 691

Scale III

Raw Score	N	%
0	179	25.9
1	151	21.9
2	166	24.0
3	101	14.6
4	71	10.3
5	16	2.3
6	7	1.0

Mean = 1.786
SD = 1.664
Median = 1.416
Mode = 1.000
Range = 0–6
N = 691

Scale IV

Raw Score	N	%
0	176	25.5
1	185	26.8
2	134	19.4
3	94	13.6
4	44	6.4
5	38	5.5
6	9	1.3
7	9	1.3
8	2	0.3

Mean = 1.725
SD = 1.463
Median = 1.593
Mode = 0.000
Range = 0–8
N = 691

Appendix 21.
Conversion of Raw Scores to Normalized T-scores for Life History Checklist (CALH) Scales

	Normalized T-Scores		
Raw Scores	Scale I	Scale III	Scale IV
0	35	39	39
1	43	47	47
2	47	52	53
3	51	58	58
4	55	64	62
5	58	70	66
6	61	76	70
7	64		74
8	67		82
9	71		
10	75		
11	82		

Appendix 22.
Sample Distribution by AIMS Group in Two Institutions (MIN and MED)

Institution	Group					Total
	I N (%)	II N (%)	III N (%)	IV N (%)	V N (%)	
MIN	172 (22.11)	100 (12.85)	273 (35.09)	213 (27.38)	20 (2.57)	778
MED	249 (34.29)	89 (12.25)	193 (26.58)	134 (18.45)	61 (8.40)	726
	421 (27.99)	189 (12.56)	466 (31.98)	347 (23.07)	81 (5.38)	1,504

Appendix 23.
Comparison of Distribution of Cases by AIMS Group: Total Sample vs. Random Sample

Institution			Group					Total
		I	II	III	IV	V		
MIN	Total N	172	100	273	213	20		778
	(% of total sample)	(22.1)	(12.9)	(35.0)	(27.4)	(2.6)		
	Random N	28	18	29	35	7		117
	(% of random sample)	(23.9)	(15.3)	(24.7)	(29.9)	(5.9)		
MED	Total N	249	89	193	134	61		726
	(% of total sample)	(34.9)	(12.3)	(26.6)	(18.5)	(8.4)		
	Random N	106	37	71	65	29		308
	(% of random sample)	(34.4)	(12.0)	(23.0)	(21.0)	(9.4)		

Appendix 24.
Comparison of Post-release Sample with Random Sample

	Group					Total
Sample	I N (%)	II N (%)	III N (%)	IV N (%)	V N (%)	
Random	134 (31.5)	55 (12.9)	100 (23.5)	100 (23.5)	36 (.08)	425
Post-release	67 (30.5)	24 (10.9)	60 (27.3)	52 (22.6)	17 (.08)	220